Magic Moments

By

Frank Pinto

Published by

Phil Hadley Publications

2025

philhadleypublications.com

Sections of this work first appeared as a series of monthly articles in the St Goran with St Michael Caerhays Parish Magazine.

ISBN 978-1-9998463-6-7

Printed by Book Printing UK

www.bookprintinguk.com

CONTENTS

Chapter		Page
	Foreward	4
1	Trewalla Farm	6
2	The Street, Gorran Haven	20
3	Disappearing Footpaths	34
4	Egg Collecting	51
5	Fishing	54
6	Fishing Marks	70
7	Weapons Of Mass Destruction	79
8	Great White Whale	84
9	Gorran Primary School	87
10	Rules To Be Broken	92
11	Guy Fawkes Night	96
12	The Flower Show	100
13	Coastguards	104
14	The Institute	109
15	Pooch's Field	112
16	Sad Times	114
17	Dick Pill Boats	118
18	Gorran Haven Crabbers	121
19	The Mildred	124
20	Wheels	128
21	Cliff Road	135
22	Foxhole Lane	142
23	Home Made Toys	147
24	Honey Bees	152
25	The Lime Kiln	156
26	Good Old Days	159
27	Boredom	170
28	Properties In Gorran Haven	175
29	My Dear Mary nee Kirken	180
30	Old Local Fishing Words	184
31	Other Old Local Words	191

FOREWARD

What follows is a series of articles I wrote and which first appeared in The Gorran and District Parish Magazine under the broad heading of HOW TIMES CHANGE. It started with, what was intended as, a one-off piece comparing Church Street in the 1950's, when I lived there, and as it was at the time of writing. After this piece was published I received a number of encouraging comments and so I decided to keep going and hope that I did not bore readers too much. This turned into a series published over a period of more than five years. It was my idea to record from my memory Gorran Haven as it was over 60 years ago and at the same time I hoped to give readers some idea as to what it was like for a young boy growing up there. I hope that I have achieved this. I really did enjoy my carefree childhood in Gorran Haven and although I no longer live there I visit very frequently and still think of it as home.

Having written these articles I thought it would be nice to put them together in a book. In this offering they are not in the order they were first published and some have been extended to include other memories which I omitted from the first edition due to lack of space in the parish magazine.

I feel I should say that these are my memories and I know that memories can play tricks. I am sure that readers who were around in Gorran Haven in the 1950's will perhaps remember things differently. I hope, however, you will still find my contribution entertaining and that it will stimulate childhood memories of your own.

Finally, I would like to say a big thank you to Phil Hadley for his very much appreciated encouragement, advice and help in getting this published.

Chapter 1.

TREWALLA FARM

(The first home I remember)

I was born in Gorran Haven in 1945 but in 1946 my mother, Mary, 16 year old brother, Ken, and I, moved with my maternal Grandparents, Tryphina and William Mingo, to Trewalla Farm. By 1949, when my brother and sister were born, we were back living in Gorran Haven with my Italian father, Pasquale, an ex POW. However my Grandparents and older brother continued to live and farm at Trewalla until 1955 by which time both of my Grandparents had died. William in 1949 and Tryphina in 1955. After moving back to Gorran Haven I continued to visit regularly, staying during school holidays and I still have many happy memories of the place.

The farm is a good mile from the nearest bus stop and I can remember walking with my mother along the country road to the farm. Me running ahead, her following with the push chair. In my memory it was always sunny. I guess we did not visit when it was raining because of the walk and the fact that we would have got soaked. When it was time to return Ken often gave us a lift to the bus stop at Rush Pool on a trailer pulled by the farm tractor. Neither family owned a car at that time.

The farm house was two fields in from the road. At that time an unsurfaced track led along the bottom hedge of the first field. As I remember it this section of the track was always full of puddles and had to be negotiated with care. This field was always cultivated. The track crossed the middle of the second field. This field was always pasture land where the milking cows grazed. Where the track left the field it turned left at a right angle and passed the farm house which was on its left. After passing the house it veered left down a short incline into a quarry from which I assume the stone was dug to build the house. In this quarry there was an ever running spring to which the cows were sometimes driven for a drink. Also in the quarry was a two storey barn used for the storage of grain and some implements. It also contained a grain crusher for converting the grain, usually Dredge Corn, a mixture of oats, wheat and barley, into animal feed.

There were also a couple of hutches in which ferrets were kept. These were used to keep down the rabbit population. This was a time before myxomatosis had been introduced.

Directly opposite the point at which the track left the field was the cobbled farm yard. This was bordered on three sides by hedges and on the upper side by farm buildings, (cow sheds and equipment sheds). I can remember the tractor, a farm cart, a hay cutter and a binder, for cutting corn, and a plough being stored there. Opposite the building in the corner of the yard there was always a large dung heap which, in the spring, was spread over the fields as fertiliser.

Beyond the farm yard was a small orchard and beyond that a steep wooded hillside at the bottom of which was a trout stream. The stream reached the sea at Caerhays. I cannot remember how many fields made up the farm but, I think, not more than 5 or 6. I do however remember spending many happy hours on the tractor driven by Ken. It was, I think, a Fordson Major. It had wide mudguards covering the rear wheels and no cab. I used to have a cushion placed behind the axle, which ran across the driving area, on which to sit. I could look up at Ken driving and watch whichever implement we happened to be towing. I clearly remember watching the sails on the binder turning when cutting corn and seeing the sheaves dropping out at the back, the clatter of the hay cutter when cutting hay and seeing the rabbits running to safety. Quite often opposite me on the tractor was a fully loaded double barrelled 12 bore shot gun when a rabbit was required for dinner.

I can remember hay making with both a tractor and a horse and the rick being built with a hay pole and a grab. The tractor had a sweep on the front, an implement with a series of long prongs, which was used to bringing the hay to the pole. The horse was used to control the grab, which ran through a pulley at the end of an arm at the top of the pole, and lifting its load onto the rick where a couple of men stood and spread the hay evenly over the surface, slowly building the rick higher and higher. Threshing was also a major event. The threshing machine was brought to the farm by a contractor and all the neighbouring farmers turned out to give a hand. I remember my Grandmother bringing out Pasties she had made for lunch and large enamel jugs of tea for all who were working.

The Farm House

As I remember it, it was a two storey building configured exactly as a child would draw a house. The front of the house had a lawned front garden divided by a central path. The front door was in the centre of the wall with a window on either side and three windows above. Inside this door was the hall with a staircase at the end. As you entered, on the left was the dining room used only on high days and holidays. Directly opposite on the right was the sitting room. Each room had an open fireplace in the centre of the wall opposite the door which burnt wood and coal. At the bottom of the staircase on the left was the doorway into the kitchen. On the right a doorway into the pantry. Directly opposite the kitchen door was the coal fired range which was used for cooking. In the outer wall of the kitchen there was one window and the back door. In front of the window, the sill of which was used as a seat was an oak topped table around which we all sat at meal times. In the walk-in pantry as well as the normal household provision there was always, I remember, an enamel bowl of clotted cream made by my grandmother.

The staircase turned to the right half way up and then right again and led onto a landing. I cannot remember the upstairs layout exactly but I believe there were four bedrooms one of which had had the window bricked up to reduce the window tax which was introduced in 1695.

There was no electricity. Lighting was obtained from candles or oil lamps. These lamps were fuelled with paraffin and had cloth wicks inside glass chimneys and were carried from room to room as required. In the 1950s these lamps were superseded by Tilly Lamps. These were lamps fuelled with paraffin which were pressurised by pumping and had mantles instead of wicks. I think they could be hung on the walls from brackets and provided much better light.

Even as a child I can remember going to bed carrying a candle in an enamel candle holder. I'm not sure what today's Health and Safety Executive would say. I also remember a china chamber pot under the bed in case of night time need.

The back door led onto a triangular courtyard which had grey slate flagstones. Directly outside the door was a pump from which household water supplies were obtained. At the end of this yard was the Chemical toilet which had to be emptied from time to time; I'm not sure where!!!. Next to the toilet there was a small room housing a milk separator. It consisted of a stack of conical weights which were spun by turning a handle. When whole milk was poured in at the top the cream was spun off and was separated from the rest of the milk. My Mother told us that when she was 16 she caught her long hair in such a machine and broke her neck. She certainly had neck problems all of her life and regularly visited an osteopath for treatment. I remember that the milk was stored in metal churns about 3ft tall which had to be trailered out to the lane entrance where they were collected daily by the milk lorry.

My Mother often told people that I used to hand milk one particular cow from the age of two. Whether the age was right I cannot say but I do remember taking a beach bucket and milking Daisy for the breakfast milk.

Rabbiting

One of the things my older brother Ken and his friends did on sunny summers evenings was to go rabbiting. Rabbits were serious pests before the introduction of myxomatosis and were also an addition to the larder. My Mother used to make a really great rabbit pie with bacon and parsley. The taste of her pies is one of my enduring childhood memories. Unfortunately I no longer have the exact recipe. The usual method for catching the rabbits was to use the ferrets. The hedges between the fields were veritable warrens and full of rabbit holes. The entrance of each hole was covered with a net and the ferret was sent into one of the holes to chase out the rabbits. Usually each side of the hedge was patrolled by someone with a 12 bore shot gun in case a rabbit bolted and escaped the nets. I was usually lifted onto the top of the hedge to walk along it to let everyone know if the ferret appeared from an un-netted hole. I can remember being very scared when a rabbit bolted and the guns were employed. When the ferret chased a rabbit into a net it was grabbed and rapidly despatched. Sometimes the ferret would catch a rabbit whilst still in its hole and would not come out, I presume staying to eat it. On these occasions there was no choice but to leave it to its own devices and return the next morning in the hope that it would still be wandering around somewhere close to where you last saw it. It usually was.

Another method used to keep the rabbit population down was to use snares. For readers not familiar with this piece of kit a snare was a sliding loop of wire attached to a stake. The stake was driven into the ground at the entrance of a rabbit hole and the wire arranged so that it formed a loop in the hole. As the rabbit left the hole it contacted the wire which tightened and held the rabbit. The more the rabbit struggled the more the loop tightened. The snares were deployed in the evening and then inspected the next morning. This was an extremely cruel way of catching anything and although I believe running snares can still be used to catch some animals their use has largely died out I am pleased to say.

Another barbaric method for catching rabbits was Gin Traps. Metal claws attached to very strong springs and held apart by a small platform. These traps were placed in the animals runs and anchored by an attached chain and spike. When the animal stepped on the platform it moved to release the spring and the jaws snapped shut clasping whatever part of the animal that was in the way, usually a leg. The animal was left in agony until someone came around much later, often the next day, to despatch it. This form of trap was quite rightly outlawed. I believe, in 1958.

At the time snares and gin traps were considered acceptable ways of pest control and I can clearly remember both being used. These examples show clearly How Times have Changed since the 1950s.

Trout Fishing

Another memory I have of my time on my Grandfather's farm was an occasion when Ken, my Father and I went trout fishing.

I mentioned that the farm house was built at the top of a steeply wooded hillside at the bottom of which was a small river. It runs through Tubbs Mill and on to Caerhays I believe. In those days there were some nice trout in the river and occasionally Ken would take me on a fishing expedition to get trout for tea. On one memorable occasion my Father, a man not known for his patience, decided to come too. Fishing rods were bamboos or lengths of hazel cut from a hedgerow with a length of hook and line tied to one end of the pole. Bait was earth worms dug from the dung heap. There was always a plentiful supply of dung in the heap in the corner of the yard next to the cow sheds.

It was a warm sunny evening and on arriving at the riverbank Ken positioned Father on an open bend in the river where he said there was the best chance of catching a nice fish. Ken and I moved further along the bank down river but still within view of Dad. Not long after lowering the bait into the water father had a catch which he proceeded to lift out of the water only for it to drop off before he got it over land. This must have happened a half a dozen times with my Father getting more and more agitated each time. The comments coming from our direction did not help. Eventually Ken walked along the bank, without taking his line out of the water, to where my father was standing. Immediately he hooked a beautiful trout which he lifted out of the river without difficulty. Having failed to land his catch on so many occasions and Ken landing his at the first attempt Father threw down his fishing pole in exasperation and stormed off.

This incident was often raised in the family as a source of amusement but I am not sure Father saw it that way. To my knowledge he never ever went fishing again either in the river or the sea.

My encounter with a Bull

One morning when I was about 5 or 6 years of age and staying at Trewalla, Ken announced that later that day we were going to take a cow to a neighbour's farm. At the time I had no idea why.

After much coaxing and not a little physical persuasion Ken managed to get the cow into a high-sided trailer which had previously been attached to the tractor and we set off. Ken driving, on his high springy metal seat, and me on my usual cushion over the tractor axle. We trundled down the road towards Tubbs Mill turning left at the bottom towards Trevenna Woods. A little way along the road on a sharp bend we turned left up a rough and narrow farm track. I am not sure if this entrance is still in use. During the journey Ken told me about how we were going to meet a huge bull emphasizing how dangerous they could be. By the time we reached the farm yard I was really frightened but trying not to show it.

I cannot remember much about the yard or farm house except for one large building. I think it had two floors. In the front centre was a deep alcove, on the left and right of which were doors into stables. The door on the right was closed but the door on the left was open and into this stable the cow was eventually directed. There was no sign of any bull and I was beginning to feel a bit more relaxed.

Then came the coup de gras. I was told to stand in the entrance of the alcove and to make sure when the bull was let out of the stable on the right that it did not escape into the yard. At this point I was petrified. Ken and his friend stood behind me after opening the stable and out came the bull. An enormous brown thing. I had no idea what to do but was not going to show my fear so stood my ground. The bull trundled across the alcove without a sideways glance into the stable occupied by the cow. The door was shut behind him. He obviously had better things to do than attack me and I had no idea, unlike Ken and his friend, that his instincts would take over. There was no such thing as artificial insemination in those days.

By 1955 when my grandmother died, Ken had married and had a 5 year old son and he gave up farming for a more regular wage working in a garage. My contact with Trewalla ended.

This was me in 1958.

Chapter 2.

THE STREET, GORRAN HAVEN.

(My first article in the Parish Magazine)

Of the 30 or so properties which line The Street (locals never referred to Church Street) only one or two are at present permanently occupied. The remainder are second homes or holiday lets. I thought readers may like to know how this differed from the early 1950s when I lived there.

Starting at the bottom of The Street on the right hand side The Mermaid Café did not exist. The area which it now occupies was an open court yard which provided access to cellars used by fishermen for storage. Above the cellars was a block of three cottages. The first had only two rooms, one above the other, and was where I lived and where my brother and sister were born in 1949. Next door to us, in the middle of the terrace, was another one up, one down cottage occupied by a Mrs Manley, a widow, and sometimes her son Victor who I think was, at that time, in the Navy. The third, 'Beach House' was bigger and in the late 1800s was the Ship Inn of Grandfather Saunders fame and once owned by Walter Hicks who founded St. Austell Brewery. I cannot remember who lived there in 1950 or whether it had already become a holiday let which it definitely did a little later. These cottages have now incorporated the cellar and the first two have been combined. Both are used for holidays.

The next property, Step Cottage, was occupied by Edwin Liddicoat and his wife Winnie. Edwin ran a smallholding in the village with his brother Alf. I think I remember them delivering milk around the village using a horse and cart. Edwin and Winnie had no children but Alf had a daughter Vera. Vera and her husband returned to the village to look after her parents when they were unable to look after themselves. She lived in Pebblebrook in Rice Lane which, I think, was built by her father in the 1930s. Vera died in 2016 over 90 years of age. Step Cottage is now a second home. Winnie died at a young age and Edwin then married a Mrs McAuliffe.

The first owners I can remember occupying the cottage behind Step Cottage and which overlooks the Platt (which did not exist in 1950) were a Mr and Mrs McGaw and their son Duncan. Duncan was a couple of years younger than me. Mr McGaw kept chickens in Quilver Close before it was developed. As well as selling eggs I think he also sold Newspapers. This cottage was once the home of the Ball family. This is now let for holidays.

The cottage now known as Pothy's Place was two properties. The ground floor was a cellar-cum- store, with a three roomed flat above it with the name of Bethel. Access to the flat was via a flight of steps on the path, which passes the church, where a flower bed now exists. I lived with my family in this flat for a short time. The two storey property which runs parallel to the church was at that time semi derelict in use as a store. I am ashamed to say my father confiscated my catapult, and that of a friend, for breaking some of the glass in the end window. When I was six or seven years of age we stood with our backs to the sea and systematically fired stones at the window. The window was made up of lots of small panes many of which were already broken. My friend did not speak to me for days after his catapult was confiscated. Interesting to note that in those days a 6 or 7 year old was allowed a catapult. Both of these properties are now used for holidays.

Above the church 'Cliff House' was occupied by Mrs Ida Coombe, a childless widow. I think her late husband was Cyrus. Ida lived in the house in the winter but in the summer moved into a chalet in the garden so that she could let the house as a vital source of income. Cliff House is still a permanent residence.

The property above Cliff House was occupied by Dave Patten and his sister Ethel, both unmarried. Dave was a local character and a full time fisherman. He had long grey hair which flowed from under his cap over his collar. He had a very old boat called the Meta. After he died it was found that the boat was virtually held together by a build-up of tar which had been enthusiastically applied annually. I think I remember her being burnt because she was considered unseaworthy. This is now a second home used by the owner for holidays.

Next was the cottage now known as Bolywinky but I cannot remember who lived there although I am told this was the home of Harriet Liddicoat. Harriet was Harry Liddicoat's mother. More of Harry later. This is now a second home and used by the owner for holidays. Bolywinky is, I think, named after a Rock but I have not been able to find anyone who knows where this rock is.

Zion Cottage comes next. I think this was owned by Mr Wellington who lived in the big house on the path to Fort next to the chapel. I only ever remember this as a holiday let which it still is.

Across the path to Fort was a block of three cottages. The first was occupied by a Miss Thomas and was called Marigold cottage. I remember Miss Thomas as an eccentric lady who wore woolly socks and cardigans which I feel sure she had knitted herself. I am told she kept a Goldfinch in a cage and often fished from the end of the quay using, as bait, worms she had dug from the beach. The next cottage was occupied by Charlie and Rita Whatty. Unfortunately I cannot remember anything about them. These two cottages have now been combined into one and is now a holiday let.

The next cottage was occupied by Florrie Dyer. Again I cannot remember anything about her. This cottage originally had no door leading directly onto the street. Access was from the path leading to Fort and behind the other two cottages. It was later purchased as a holiday home, I think in the 50's, by Sir Hugh Park, an eminent QC. I am not sure if it was he who put in the present doorway. Sir Hugh was a great friend to the Fishermen's Society and did a lot of legal work for them. Although Sir Hugh is no longer alive, I believe the property remains within the family and is still used as a holiday home.

Of the 15 properties mentioned 14 were permanently occupied. Today only one is.

Starting again at the bottom of The Street on the left, the cottage on the corner was occupied by Charlie Billing, an old, retired seafarer, I think. Charlie was the father of Lewis Billing, of which more later. Charlie had a very broad Cornish accent which I found difficult to understand but which I found fascinating. He used to wait on the Lime Kiln for Lewis to return from fishing and I, as a small child, used to engage him in conversation just to hear him speak. I am sure I used to nod and shake my head in all of the wrong places. This cottage is now used for holidays.

The next cottage was occupied by Will Juleff and his wife Seiny (my spelling). Seiny was Charlie's sister but I have been told following some family rift they never spoke to each other. I think by the time I remember him Will was retired. Will had a big bushy moustache. I remember an occasion when a friend came in from a fishing trip saying that he had seen a seal. This was a rare occurrence at that time. As I had then never seen one, in those days nobody had a TV to enlighten us, I asked what it looked like. The answer I got was 'Will Juleff'. This cottage is a holiday home.

Both of these cottages are accessed from the alley at the back.

A partially covered yard comes next behind a high wall with an access door onto the street. This was used by Harry Liddicoat as a workshop and store and housed his small boat in the winter. Harry, I think, was a carpenter and painter and decorator. He lived at 2 Cliff Close opposite the Coastguard Cottages. It was Harry's mother who lived in Bolywinky.

The first person I remember living in the next cottage on the corner of Rattle Street was Granny Cakebread, a widow. Everyone will know her Granddaughter Barbara who still owns and runs the village store. This is now a holiday home.

On the opposite corner of Rattle Street the cottage was occupied by Granny Patten, a widow. Her Granddaughter and one of her grandsons still live in the village. This is now a holiday home.

The next cottage was the home of Henry Johns, his wife Jessica and their son Eric. Jessica's uncle, Tommy Billing, also lived with them. He was a reclusive man, rarely seen. He originally owned the Lime Kiln and gave it to the parish council so that the public would for ever have access to it. Henry was a fisherman who worked with his brothers on a boat called "The Pet" which operated out of Mevagissey. They mainly fished for Pilchards like most of the other Mevagissey boats at the time. Their catches were canned in the Mevagissey fish factory which was then at the bottom of Tregony Hill. This cottage is now a holiday home.

These last two cottages share a small triangular courtyard at the back.

Carrie Liddicoat lived in the next three storey cottage with her husband Jake. Their son Phil also lived in the village at that time in Foxhole Lane with his wife Betty (nee Burns). This cottage is also a holiday home.

Adjoining this cottage was another. Three rooms one above the other. At one time a couple named Ford lived there but I cannot remember if they were there in 1950. I do, however, remember a Mrs Hall living there after her husband Nobby, a coastguard, died. This must have been several years later. This cottage is now a holiday let.

There are three cottages in the alleyway that follows. The first was occupied by Miss Coombe, a nice old spinster lady. She was semi-invalid and I believe was Ida's sister-in-law. My mother used to clean for her and sometimes I went with her. Miss Coombe used to entertain me and give me books. One I remember was a Penguin paperback about working elephants in Burma which I found fascinating. This is now used for holidays.

I cannot remember who lived in the inner cottage but am told it was the home of Phil Tom Guy. It is possible that by 1950 it was a holiday home as it is now.

The third cottage has a front garden and then had a cellar below. It was occupied by Lewis Billing and his wife Miriam. They had no children. Lewis was a fisherman and his boat the Coral Reef is still in the village and is over 90 years old. She was built by Dick Pill in the yard which is now occupied by the chip shop and the Beachcomber. Lewis's second boat, which he had built at Porthleven, was also called the Coral Reef. She was built by the Oliver Brothers and has returned to a new owner in the port in which she was built. This cottage is now used for holidays.

The next cottage was in fact a village shop run by Mr. Tubb whose son still lives in the village. Mr Tubb later moved this shop to the building which is now the Chip Shop. This is now used for holidays.

The next cottage, I am told, was the home of Leonie Teague who was a sister of John Teague who was the headmaster at Gorran School for many years and taught me and got me through the 11-Plus. In 1950 this property was empty and shortly after became a holiday let although it is now permanently occupied.

Will and Elizabeth Pollard lived in the next property. Elizabeth was Swiss born and was always affectionately known as 'Swissy Pollard'. They had no children. Will was a fisherman and his boat was the Albion which is still in the village. This cottage is now used for holidays. Elizabeth often looked after my brother and sister when they were toddlers when my mother was out cleaning.

Bertram Pollard and his wife Ethel lived in the next cottage, "Wrens Nest". They had no children. Bertram was a fisherman working with Will Ball in a boat called Cotswold which was also built by Dick Pill in 1921. Will Ball lived next door to Harry Liddicoat opposite the coastguard cottages. Bertram had a very badly burn-scarred face as a result of an accident during the Second World War. I remember him as a large quiet man. The Cotswold was later replaced by a brand new bigger boat which they had built, called the Fulmar. Unfortunately this boat was lost when caught at anchor by the outer step. An unexpected storm blew up driving waves over the quay which ran off into the boat, swamping it. She was completely broken up and, if I remember correctly, the only part found was the engine. I think this was in the autumn of 1957 or 58. Bertram never went to sea again whilst Will Ball returned to fishing on his own in his original boat the Cotswold which is still in the village. I believe a little later Henry Johns crewed for Will in the

Cotswold and when Will retired Henry fished in this boat alone. This is now used for holidays. Bertram was Granny Patton's brother.

The last house at the top of the street on the left was occupied by two spinster sisters, Liza and Aida Harvey. I think they must have been fairly reclusive as I can remember nothing about them. A friend tells me however that as you passed they always asked what time it was. I also remember that Will and Elizabeth Pollard eventually moved into this property. I am not sure whether to look after the sisters in their old age or after they died. This property is still permanently occupied.

As can be seen in the 1950's of the 14 properties mentioned 12 were continuously occupied. Today only 2 are. I guess this change is reflected throughout Cornwall. How times change. As you all know, I was but a child in 1950 and memories can play tricks. I have recorded this in good faith and hope that this piece does not contain too many inaccuracies.

NOTE

Another sister of Charlie Billing was Mrs Julia Lafette. Mr and Mrs Lafette lived at Sea Way next to Cakebread's shop in the ground floor of the Customs House. A Jacob Billing lodged with them but I do not know if, or how, he was related.

Finally, as properties are continually changing hands and people move residences the ownership and occupation of these properties may have changed since this was written. However the situation does, I am sure, remain the same in that very few of these properties are permanently occupied.

The Street from a 1939 Tuck's postcard.

Chapter 3.

DISAPPEARING FOOTPATHS

(Never to return)

The Huers Path

By 1953, and the time of the Coronation, I was living in a Coastguard Cottage. The council had just taken over half of the Board of Trade's coastguard properties for council housing following a reduction in the number of coastguards employed in the village.

In 1953 the site now occupied by "Dolphins Leap" was a vegetable patch and chicken run. I cannot remember who tended it. What I do remember is that we kids always referred to this area as Pardon Gates not Parc-en-Gates as it is now. I have no idea why. Immediately above the entrance to "Benvista" was a footpath running between the boundaries of the two properties and along in front of "Blue Point" and ending in front of "Caprera" where the cliff had fallen away. This path was used by fishermen when seining, mostly I think for Pilchards, Mullet or Bass.

From this path was an uninterrupted view down into the bay below. A fisherman (a Huer) was sent to this path to look for shoals of fish. When any were spotted he would signal to the other fishermen below, waiting in the seine boat, that it was time to shet (deploy) the net. This was rowed out from the beach around the shoal and back to the beach where it was pulled in with its catch. I can clearly remember standing on this path with Lewis Billing looking down on the seine boat below. I cannot remember the catch, if there was one. By this time the seine was rarely used as large shoals had largely disappeared. When it did come out it caused us kids much excitement.

On one occasion I can remember the seine being deployed on the main beach and catching nothing but a large salmon. It was out of the salmon season and illegal to land. John Ball, the son of Will Ball and then a London policeman, was home on holiday and watching proceedings. The fish was dutifully returned to the sea. I still wonder what would have happened had John not been there.

Parc-an-Gates

Almost directly opposite the Huers path just described was another which no longer exists.

This started on the left of the hill at Parc-en-Gates and ran along the bottom of the field which now forms part of Perhaver Park. It followed the boundaries of, what at that time were, the back gardens of the Coastguard cottages, and is now occupied by the old peoples' bungalows. On the right of this path, at the bottom of the field, was a row of allotments. I have a story about a Bee hive kept in one of these allotments which I will keep for a later date. At the end of the field it turned left and ended roughly where the stream runs under the road in Perhaver Park between the properties of 22 and 24.

At the end of this lane was a gateway into the first of two fields between this gate and Trewollock Lane. These fields were farmed by Alf and Edwin Liddicoat. From 1953 to 1970 I lived in one of the coastguard cottages and as a small child regularly climbed through the back hedge into this lane, because, not far from the field gate, were a couple of small ponds from which we collected frogs, newts and tadpoles. These ponds would have been roughly where the bungalow at No. 22 now stands. At the top of the same field were a number of other small ponds. These never contained any wildlife. I think this was because they were fed by continually running natural springs. I remember the water was always very clear and contained no pond weed.

At the end of the lane, on the right as you faced the fields, was a withy (willow) orchard. This was roughly opposite where No.24 now stands and ran all the way to the top boundary. These withies were harvested annually by the fishermen who at that time made their own crab pots. These pots rarely lasted more than one season and new ones were made during the winter when no fishing was possible. The stumps left after cutting looked like rows of giant mushrooms. These stumps were referred to by the local fishermen as "Motts". Where this word originates I have no idea and may be just a Gorran Haven term. These withies were also the source of material from which all the local boys made their bows and arrows.

Suez

Another path which has disappeared is the one we all described as "Suez". This ran from Foxhole Lane, parallel to Canton to the steps which still exist opposite "Harbours Reach". I can only assume it was named after the canal.

In the 50s the bank opposite the hairdressers was overhanging and a row of trees grew along its top edge. Suez ran between these trees and the garden fences of the bungalows which are still there. As kids we regularly used this path and often climbed the trees along it. I believe the path was originally used by residents of Foxhole Lane, as a short cut to a pump, at a time when their properties had no running water. The remains of this pump, I think, still exist opposite "Harbours Reach".

This path was lost when the trees were removed and the bank re-contoured. I assume Health and Safety played its part.

The entrance to this path was immediately below Harbour View where Frank Guy, a fisherman and local character lived with his wife Ruby and daughter Glennis. Frank fished with his brother Monro in a boat called the Velsheda.

Immediately after this house was a small Bark House. A small building which housed a coal fired boiler in which fishermen boiled their lines and ropes in some potion to preserve them from the effects of seawater. In those days the ropes were made from natural fibres. There was a line of these houses along the wall on Driving Boats by the second set of steps leading to The Institute (Village Hall). Unfortunately all of these have long since been demolished. Next to the Bark House along Suez was the entrance to a Withy Orchard. This was another source of sticks for bows and arrows as well as for crab pots. This area was eventually developed by a man, locals always referred to as Johnny Hopeless, not his real name I'm sure. He lodged in the village with Jack Henna and his wife in a bungalow now called Tickety Boo which is just after the top of Church Street on the right. He had three Cornish Unit bungalows built on this withy orchard. This development I have been told resulted in Foxhole Lane being improved and tarmacked. Before then, the part above Suez was nothing more than a wide path down which water poured when it rained.

The bungalow next to the withy orchard was owned by the Clarke family as a holiday home. We always believed they were of Clarke Shoe fame but I do not know if this was true. They kept a pleasure boat in Big Cellars. Each Year they held a film show in The Institute where they showed the cine films that they had taken on their previous holidays both in Gorran Haven and abroad. A much looked forward to event in the 50's before anyone in the village had a TV.

The next bungalow was occupied by a gentleman who lived alone. I could not remember his name but am told it was a Mr Bell. He stays in my memory because he owned a Victorian display cabinet with lots of thin drawers. This contained a properly laid out collection of butterflies of the world. On occasions we were invited in to view them. We were all very impressed. There was no such thing in those days as stranger danger.

The next bungalow was occupied by Ern Liddicoat who lived with his sister Mary Martin and her two grown up sons Alan and Christopher. Ern owned and ran a garage and filling station at Menagwins where the terrace of houses is now. Ern had a reputation for being a bit mean but I liked him. He had a very dry sense of humour. By 1965 I was working in St. Austell and travelling by motorbike. I remember one occasion on my way home from work on a Thursday evening, the day before I received my £4 10s wage. I stopped for petrol. Ern came out to serve me. No self-service in those days. I asked him for half a gallon. All I could afford until I got paid. He paused before picking up the nozzle and said, "Don't ee want to get 'ome boy". He knew I lived only a mile down the road. I think half a gallon was about 1s 3d (6.5p) at the time. After owning and farming some of the land Ern was later involved with the development of Perhaver Park together with Frank Lobb a local builder.

Big Perhaver Path

Another footpath which has disappeared since I was a kid is the one which led from the field at the end of Cliff Road down to Big Perhaver beach.

Unfortunately the cliff at the top fell away, I think in the early 1980's, which now prevents its use. This was a very easy path to negotiate having no really steep bits in it. When we were small we used to enjoy clambering over the rocks at low tide from Little Perhaver to Big Perhaver and returning via this path when the tide prevented return via the rocks. We used to explore the beach and boulders, almost as far as Pabyer Hole, to see what the sea had brought in. I can remember one bright sunny morning when we found, along the water's edge, lots of tiny cuttle fish or squid, I'm not sure which. They were alive, perfectly formed and would fit easily into the palm of a 10 year olds hand. A real wonder of nature. After this every visit to Big Perhaver involved a search for these little creatures. Unfortunately to this day the experience has never been repeated.

When we got older Big Perhaver was occasionally the venue for late night or all night parties. We would collect drift wood during the day for a bonfire in the evening. Someone would take a guitar and much alcohol was transported, usually bottles of sweet Spanish Sauterne and flagons of triple vintage cider. (More alcoholic and less to carry than bottles of beer). For these occasions we were usually ferried over by boat but returned via the path.

After South Easterly gales many locals would use this path to collect drift wood. Sometime good enough for reuse in construction, garden sheds and the like, but more often as fire wood. In the 50's very few properties had any form of central heating relying on open coal fires. Any free wood came in very handy. If the "treasure" found was too much to carry back in one trip it was then the practise to pile up your bounty in a heap above the high water line. This neatly stacked heap told all later "wreckers" that this had been claimed and was awaiting later collection. No one ever pilfered these heaps leaving them to the original finders. I cannot imagine this happening today.

Half way up the path on the right was, and still is I believe, a small withy orchard. I am not sure which of the old fishermen planted this.

Not long ago when I waded around to Big Perhaver I noticed that the sea had eroded away the bottom of the path. It now looks as if access from both top and bottom is no longer available. On this visit we were accompanied by two seals. As we waded back from the far end of the beach they followed, only a short distance from us, all the way back to Fort Point before submerging and disappearing. A really nice experience.

It is a shame that there is now no access to this beach other than by boat, unless you want to risk getting cut off by the tide.

Recently a couple of memories came to me relating to one of these beach parties which I thought I would record.

It would have been about 1960 during the school summer holidays. It was usual to get to the beach on these occasions by boat. A friend would make several ferrying trips. One of the incidents I remembered related to this boat at the end of the evening. It should be remembered that much drink had been consumed by this time. Two or three young ladies decided it was time to return home.

The boat was brought ashore and was duly loaded. On pushing off from the beach it was lifted on a larger than normal wave and as the wave went past it was partially deposited onto a submerged rock close to the steel pier. The result was that the boat listed violently throwing its contents, the young ladies and my friend, half out of the boat. There was much screaming and confusion for a short time but the next wave lifted the boat back into the sea and normality was resumed. All were lucky to have stayed aboard.

The second incident relates to a young lady that I accompanied that night. This friend lived out of the village and had arranged for her father to collect her from the Lime Kiln at midnight. The evening was spent sitting around the bonfire. Some people baking freshly caught mackerel but all drinking. As mentioned before usual tipples being sweet Spanish sauterne and triple vintage cider in double handled flagons obtained from Llawnroc: more alcoholic and less to carry than bottles of beer. I don't think that cans of beer had been invented then. When the time came to leave we set out up the cliff path. It soon became very evident that my friend was seriously affected by what had been consumed during the evening. The path was partially overgrown and was quite dark. Very soon my friend could only progress on her hands and knees with me helping with the occasional push from behind. Frequently she had to dive into the undergrowth at the side of the path to throw up. Eventually, and after what seem like hours, we made it to the top and climbed over the style into the field and into the moonlight. I looked at my friend and saw that she had stuck to her cheek one of those really large yellow slugs. She had had no idea.

Oh the pleasure of youth.!!

Vault

Another cliff path which has disappeared since the 1950's is the one which used to go over the top of Pen-a-maen point en route to Vault. The path from Gorran Haven to Vault beach used to go straight on where it now turns left towards Pen-a-maen point. Access to the point was then a spur.

Although this path involved a bit of a scrabble up between the rocks it was the one most regularly used. At this point there is a plaque, (see below) attached to one of the vertical rocks, in honour of Sir John Fischer Williams who owned Lamledra House which looks out over Vault beach. After the war Miss Rapson who had come to the village with the evacuees from the Priory School in Hayling Island ran a school in the house. The house I believe is still owned by the family. It is my understanding that Sir John donated the coastal land between Gorran Haven and the Dodman to the National Trust.

At the top of the climb the path descended diagonally towards Vault until it joined the current path running along the cliff edge. Also at the top of the climb it was possible to turn right onto another path and follow it up to the old coastguard Look Out, now long gone. This was a cedar-wood hut with large windows. Coastguards were employed all year round to sit in this hut scouring the bay for potential shipping disasters. Originally the hut was manned 24 hours a day later reduced to bad weather watches only. This is hard to imagine in this time of radar and satellites and modern communications. The path went on past the hut to Lamledra House eventually joining the road at the top of Lamledra Hill. My memory of this path is that it was usually quite overgrown, up to the Look Out, through lack of use. The Coastguards usually accessed the Look Out via Lamledra Hill. At the end of this path behind the farm buildings and just before it joined the road there used to be a large pond.. I can remember being chased by geese as I passed this pond. Very scary for us young kids.

The plaque, mentioned above, reads:-

"In Memory of
JOHN FISCHER WILLIAMS
Knight. CBE KC
Of Lamledra in this Parish
Sometime Scholar and Fellow of
New College Oxford
Born 1870 – died 1947

International jurist and man of letters
A lover of his country and of this place

Upright faithful constant and most just
He sought not his own advancement
But strove ardently that under the rule of law
Peace might be established amongst all nations."

Note:

Since writing this the path to Vault described above has been reinstated to roughly it original route.

Rope Walk

Rope Walk was another route which exists no longer. Whilst not strictly a footpath, was used by locals as a short cut from one side of the village to the other.

This path started opposite, what is now, The Llawnroc Hotel, the gateway still exists between two bungalows. It crossed the field, which has now been developed, towards the carpark and then ran along the top boundary of the carpark, down into a small valley behind Rice Farm and exited where the current entrance to Mariners is now. As you can see it cut off the walk around beach corner.

In case anyone is tempted to walk this route I hasten to say that there is now no through access as the field at the end has been developed. The name Rope Walk I believe comes from the time when ropes were made locally and were made here. Rope Walk provided a flat straight area on which, I presume, ropes could be laid out and stretched.

Another short cut I remember but also not technically a footpath was up through The Meadow, the name we all used in the 50's for the Allotments. The route ran from the corner of Rattle Street to the top of The Meadow and exited via a small gate just opposite and below the entrance to the coastguard station. This gate has been removed since the development at the top.

Chapter 4.

EGG COLLECTING

(Popular then, but illegal now)

Around 1955 I did what all boys living in the countryside did at that time. I collected bird's eggs. This hobby is now illegal but I am convinced that we did very little harm, usually taking only one egg from each clutch we found. I can still remember where each egg was found, a Long Tailed Tit's from Slips, a Chiff-Chaff's from Llawnroc, and a Robin's from Cooks Level, a Dunnocks from outside Pabyer in Cliff Road and so on. The Observer Books were our source of information on birds, eggs and any other subject we were interested in. Egg collecting generated an interest in birds which has remained with me to this day.

There was one occasion when we broke our rule of one egg per clutch. This was when we found a Kestrel's nest. On a sunny spring evening three friends and I were walking along the path which led down to Pen-a-Maen point. Of these friends one still lives in the village, one went to live in Australia and unfortunately I lost touch with the third, Paul, when he left the village with his brother and mother in the late 50s. It was Paul's mother who was responsible for opening Llawnroc, first as a members club, and later as a Pub.

We saw the Kestrel fly out from under the cliff edge and decided to investigate. The cliff edge was at the bottom of a steepish grassy slope and we decided that if we lay face down on the grass, one behind the other, holding the ankles of the one in front, one of us could safely look over the edge. Paul volunteered to be the one on the cliff edge. We lay down one behind the other and shuffled forward. When he got to the edge not only could Paul see the nest with one egg in it but he could also reach it. This caused much consternation because there were four of us and only one egg. Not only that but no one person could safely get to the nest without the aid of the other three. After much debate it was decided not to tell anyone of our find and return, after school, the next day to see if more eggs had been laid. The next day there were two and by the fourth day there were four. I am slightly ashamed to say we each had one. It was such a prize that our "one per clutch" rule had to be ignored!!!!

I also remember checking gulls eggs to see if they were addled, usually from nests behind the quay. It was possible to tell by shaking them. If they sounded thin and watery they were addled and we knew that they would never develop and that when opened they would stink. We used to throw them at each other as stink bombs. The pleasures of children!!!

In pursuit of our hobby we walked miles, learnt much about the local birds and their habitats and spent all of our spare time in the open air. Healthy and happy. No TV or computer games to get in the way.

Robin's eggs in the nest.

Chapter 5.

FISHING

(Professional and Very Amateur)

I have mentioned some fishermen in earlier items but thought it might be interesting to list those I remember from the 1950s. I remember 9 boats working full time out of Gorran Haven with some 12 people making a living from the sea.

The fishermen I remember were:-

Henry Hunkin lived with his wife and daughter in Mentone, the bungalow opposite Blue Point in Cliff Road. His boat was the Jean.

Will Ball lived in Beachcliff, opposite the coastguard station, and fished with Bertram Pollard who lived in Wrens Nest at the top of the street (Church Street). Their boat was the Cotswold although they later had a brand new boat built called the Fulmar. Unfortunately the Fulmar was lost when a storm blew up unexpectedly and she was caught at anchor by the outer steps. After the

Fulmar was lost Bertram retired and Will went back to fishing from the Cotswold. Will was a quiet man who often wore a jacket and always a flat cap. I seem to remember he chewed tobacco rather than smoke it. He always kept a twist (a length of twisted tobacco which looked a bit like a piece of twisted liquorice) inside the headband of his cap. When required a plug was cut from it with his pocket knife. Other fishermen smoked the same tobacco in their pipes. In this case the plug was rubbed in the palm of the hand to loosen it up before filling the pipe.

Dave Patten lived with his sister in the street just up from the church. I remember him with white hair sticking out from under a black cap. His boat was the Meta. She was very old and virtually held together with tar. When he died, I think I remember, his boat being burnt as she was not considered seaworthy. I remember him looking out of his cottage with his elbows on the bottom half of the stable door.

Will Pollard lived in the street almost opposite Dave Patten with his Swiss born wife Elizabeth. His boat was the Albion.

Lewis Billing lived with his wife Miriam in a house down the alley opposite the church. His boat was the Coral Reef. Lewis also had a new boat built in the late 50s also called the Coral Reef. The newer boat is now operating out of Porthleven whilst the original is still in Gorran Haven.

Fred Liddicoat and his brother Jim lived in Rattle Street with Jim's wife Dorrie. Their boat was the Lindy Lou. Fred was a chain smoker of untipped Woodbines.

Maurice Patten lived with his parents in the last but one cottage at the end of Rattle Street called Veronica Cottage. His boat was the Ismeer. Later he too had a new, much smaller, boat built which he named the Joanne. His father was always known as Boxer Patten. I don't know why as his real name was John. His wife was called Mary.

The brothers Frank and Monro Guy owned the Velsheda. Frank lived with his wife and daughter in Foxhole Lane whilst Monro lived with his wife and two daughters in Elmsdale opposite the car park. Monro later moved with his family into a bungalow, Shangri-La, which he had built in Lamledra Hill

In addition there was Henry Johns who lived in the Street with his wife Jessica and son Eric. Henry originally fished from Mevagissey with his brothers on a pilchard driver called The Pet. After the Fulmar was lost and Bertram retired, Henry joined Will Ball in the Cotswold and later bought the Ismeer from Maurice Patten and fished alone.

As well as the Coral Reef, also still in the village are Ismeer, Cotswold and Albion. All now used for pleasure fishing. These 3 boats were built in Gorran Haven in the early 1900s by Dick Pill whose boat yard was where the Chippy and Beach Comber now stand.

Unfortunately all but two of these fishermen were either childless or had daughters so as these men retired full time fishing almost died out. It is however good to see there is now at least one boat working out of the village keeping the tradition alive.

Most of the fishermen already mentioned fished for crab and lobster with their homemade withy pots and in the 1950s also fished for conger eel and dogfish using longlines containing hundreds of hooks. I can still see these lines in The Pound neatly coiled in withy mawns (large withy baskets) with the hooks stuck into strips of corks, which were tied to the rim of the mawn, to stop them getting tangled. When baited, usually with bits of mackerel but sometimes salted squid/cuttlefish, the hooks were hung over the side of the mawn in exactly the right order for shetting.

The catch was usually brought ashore during mid-morning and during school holidays and on Saturdays we kids used to look forward to seeing who had caught what. The catch was usually gutted on the quay and the dogfish skinned. As conger eels are cannibals, big fish eating smaller ones whole, we were always excited to see what had been devoured. How sad is that! I am sure that on more than one occasion a recent meal was released still alive. I think, as it was not long after the war, all fish found a market and we were always told that the congers were used to make Shiphams' fish paste. A popular sandwich filler of the time, sold in small glass screw top, jars which I was recently surprised to see are still available in Tesco. The dogfish, I think, were sold as Rock Salmon or Huss to fish and chip shops.

At that time the Gorran Haven fishermen had their own co-op and used the garage opposite the Chippy, and a little later the building on the Limekiln which is now the Doctors surgery, to accumulate their catches before sending them to market.

I can remember one morning when a thick sea mist had descended and all the boats had returned except for Henry Hunkin. The other fishermen waited on the end of the quay for him to return. The atmosphere was not one of panic but certainly there was concern that Henry was not back. Eventually the sound of an engine could be heard and a boat appeared in the gloom. "Where am I,?" came a shout, across the water. "Portloe" was the immediate reply from the quay. Upon which the boat went about and disappeared into the mist. I am pleased to say it returned about ten minutes later no worse for the joke. I always found it strange that in spite of the concern that one of their number was missing they could still play this trick.

I was never much of a fisherman but living in a fishing village and having free run of the beach as soon as I started school, and possibly before, it was impossible not to have some interest in fish, even if only to eat.

As 4 or 5 year old kids the first fish we caught were Garlips (Blennies), rock pool fish, usually dark brown in colour, with largish heads and big lips which could grow to about 3 inch long. I think they could change colour to match their surroundings so were sometimes mottled green. The easiest way of catching these was at low tide from crevices in the rocks where the fish congregated to await the return of the sea. The technique was to use the thin end of a withy, discarded from crab pot making, and always available outside Big Cellars, to poke into the crevice to winkle out the fish. Garlips bite and could give a 5 year old quite a nasty nip. In fact if you fed the tail of one to the mouth of another it was possible to build a chain of two or three fish. After catching they were returned to a nearby pool for catching another day.

A favourite crevice exists in the rocks below Fort. It is situated behind an overhanging rock and could be relied upon to house several fish. A few summers ago I took my 6 year old great nephew Ben to see if the fish were still there. Because of my considerable bulk there was no way I could get into a position to see into this crevice. In fact I could not even see the crevice which I know is there. It made me realise just how young we must have been when we caught these fish. Unfortunately Ben was too scared to squeeze between the rocks to look. The fact that he had just been attacked by an Alsatian may have had something to do with his anxiety.

As we got a little older we progressed to *rod and line.* The rod being a length of withy, the line being a length of gut found on the beach and the hook being a bent dress-makers pin. Hooks were not allowed by my parents because of the barb which would prevent removal in the event that some part of our anatomy got accidentally impaled. Bait was usually the inside of a muscle or the innards of a limpet.

A favourite pool in which to use this equipment was also on Fort Point. About two thirds of the way along the point and about four feet up from sand level there is a smallish pool about 18 inches deep. It is at the bottom of what I can only describe as a three sided chimney. In the middle of this pool is a rock which protrudes above the water. If you are small enough you can squeeze into the chimney and stand on the rock. From this position it is possible to dangle the bait by the side of the stone under which the Garlips sheltered. Surprisingly we did sometimes make a catch although mostly the fish fell off before they could be lifted out of the pool.

Other targets of our attention were eels. By crawling up the river, outside the Mermaid Café, under the road and turning over debris, such as old hessian sacks and pieces of cardboard brought down by the river it was possible to catch handfuls of baby eels. They were about 3 inch long and had the diameter of parcel string. They were brownish black in colour. I have no idea if they are still there or what they grew into and I am certainly not now going to crawl up the river to find out. I suppose I should say that in the 1950s the portion of the river at the end of the building was not covered as it is today. It was then possible to crawl under the road.

Shore crabs were other targets. These could always be found, buried in the sand, at the base of the rocks over by Red Rock or under the boulders behind the quay. Under these boulders it was also possible to find Sucker Fish, Pipe Fish, Garlips and Rockling as well as the crabs. Unfortunately recent expeditions have turned up practically nothing. I am assuming that since the clean-up of the sewage system, a food source has disappeared and the wildlife has moved somewhere more to their liking. I find the disappearance of this wildlife slightly upsetting but as the young locals of today probably have absolutely no interest in what is on our beach I don't suppose it matters. I suppose the upside is that the sea must now be healthier to swim in.

By the time we reached the ripe old age of 7 or 8 (1952/53) our ambitions had grown and we had progressed to hand lines with floats and proper hooks and were fishing from the end of the quay. Boats were, for me, still not allowed. In exchange for the unsupervised freedom I was given there were rules laid down by those indoors. No rock climbing, no boating until I could swim. Home in time for every meal, and in my case, having to wear a red beret so that I could be seen and identified from a distance. My friend had to wear his father's red Probus School cap. I'm sure we all agree that rules are there to be broken but that is a story for another occasion.

By this time bait was usually white rag worms dug from the beach at low tide, mostly from Little Perhaver but also from Rock Beach. At this age beach spades and buckets were the tools of choice. I used to really enjoy those sunny mornings with the sun glinting off the wet unmarked sand. If we were very lucky we could sometimes dig up live sand eels (which we called Sprats) that had been caught out by the receding tide and had buried in the sand. It was possible to catch these simply by stamping on the sand and they would come flapping to the surface.

The fish we caught from the quay were mostly small Pollock about 6 inches long and in the summer at high tide we caught Smelt. These fish used to swim about a foot below the surface in shoals of about ten or a dozen and were easily spotted and it seemed were always eager to take the bait. Smelt are small silver fish about six inches long and almost round in circumference. I think I heard on the radio the other day that they are now considered to be an endangered species. Any catch was considered a great prize and my mother used to fry both species for me, almost to a crisp, and serve them on toast.

If we wanted a bit more sport we fished for wrasse using shore crab as bait. These were found under rocks behind the quay. These fish fought hard but were returned after catching as they were considered no good for eating.

When we got a little older (10 to 12) and had learnt to swim and had access to rowing boats we progressed to a little more serious fishing. We shet spilters, a line with 20 or 30 hooks. These were laid just below low water mark along the beach and retrieved at high tide. The target fish were anything flat, plaice, sole, turbot etc. I don't remember having great success with this technique. We plummeted for mackerel which in those days were always available and we towed a line around the coast hoping for a bass.

In the Summer we also went spear fishing. We all had goggles and snorkels and a broom handle with a straightened conger hook bound to the end. We wore T-shirts which we thought kept us from getting too cold and we dived to the bottom to spear any flatty we saw. It is amazing how much bigger things look through goggles. This pastime lost its interest after my brother got accidentally speared in the corner of his eye and had to be taken to the doctor to have the hook cut out.

I can remember fishing from a boat at dusk just off Pen-a-Maen point for what we called Chad but which I think were sea bream. These were available in very large numbers. I think they were used as crab pot bait although a few were eaten. I seem to remember that they contained masses of very fine bones and large tough scales so were not my favourite.

Fisherman Fred Liddicoat.

In the late 50's squid or cuttle fish (I am not sure which they were) were salted down to be used, at the start of the new season, as crab pot bait. These were caught in the autumn and I can remember rowing through The Pool in the September moonlight with a friend in charge of the line. The technique was to bait the line with a whole mackerel. The squid would latch onto the bait. The line was pulled slowly to the side of the boat and the squid was gaffed in a downward strike. The idea was that the fish would eject its ink into the sea, not your face, and was then safe to bring into the boat. This was only partially successful as, as soon as it had got rid of its ink, it filled up with water. This it squirted all over those of us in the boat. I can remember getting very wet.

By the time I reached 15 or 16 fishing got even more serious. I crewed for a friend who had a boat with an outboard motor and after school and at weekends we fished for conger eel. We had a long line with about 120 hooks which were baited with mackerel and which was usually shet at the back of Pen-a-Maen point. The conger we caught we gave to Lewis Billing. In exchange he sold us medium size crab at fish market wholesale prices, which at that time was nine old pence each or about four new pence. We sold these crabs on to holiday makers and Llawnroc at half a crown each or twelve and a half new pence. A considerable profit which I am slightly ashamed to say kept us in beer and cigarettes. Beer was about 1s and 6d a pint (about 9p) and I think cigarettes were about the same for 20 tipped Woodbines. It would be nice to be able to get these items at these prices today.

My connection with fishing ended when I started full time work in 1963 and discovered girls. I no longer had time for going to sea.

Rob Holland and the writer circa 1960. Not all of our catch was this big.

Chapter 6.

FISHING MARKS

(Visible locations used for triangulation)

Fort Point, Red Rock, Big Perhaver Point and Turbot point

Ever since fishermen took their boats to sea they had their favourite " Marks" - places where they felt they had the best chance of catching a Lobster or Pollack etc. Each fisherman had his own favourite marks and as they were greatly prized they were kept secret. One fisherman would not tell another in case he lost an advantage and as a result I feel sure many of these marks have been lost as each of the old fisherman has passed on. Before satellite navigation and fish finders and as it is not always possible to see the sea bed a system of triangulation was used to enable the fisherman to return repeatedly to the same spot. This involved lining up at least three visible land-based objects. In other words "Landmarks". The land based objects were given names which I know are being forgotten so before they disappear altogether I thought I would record as many as I and my friends can remember. I feel I should also say that many of these landmarks have more than one name. Mevagissey and Gorran Haven fishermen often had different names for the same places, as did different families within the village. At this point I feel I should also apologise for my spelling of rock names. In most cases I have no idea what the correct spelling should be but I have done my best.

Although I am sure they are known to all, I will, for the record, start with the names of the local beaches. Standing at the beach entrance and looking out to sea the section to the right (starboard) of the river, never ever referred to as a stream, is **Boat Beach**, for obvious reasons. To the left (port) is **Rock Beach**. Then comes **Little Perhaver** and then **Big Perhaver**, never Great to locals. Then around the point and not visible from the beach entrance is **Colona**. On the other side of the bay is **Pen-a-Maen Point**, sometimes know as Maenease. Around Pen-a-Maen and just before **Vault** (sometimes referred to as Bow Beach but never by locals), which I am sure everyone knows, is **Little Sands**. This is accessed by climbing down the cliff or over the rocks from the entrance to Vault. At the very end of Vault where the Dodman (Deadman) starts is **Penveor Cove.**

Now for the cliffs and rocks. The point to the left of Rock Beach is **Fort Point** with the Fort cottages on it. Across Little Perhaver is **Blue Point** not much of a point but made up of blue shale rock and with the new building of the same name above it. Next along the coast is **Red Rock** ironically more of a point than a rock but of a reddish colour. The building above also has the same name. Around Red Rock and only accessible at low tide is the cave. When we were kids we always referred to it as **Johnny Paveman's Hole**. I have also heard it called Johnny Pateman's Hole and Johnny Paintman's Hole.

Which is correct I have no idea but it seems he was called Johnny. I have no idea who this gentleman was but it would be nice to think he was a local smuggler or pirate.

Next comes **Big Perhaver Point** separating the two beaches. Just around the point is a large rock which dries out at low tide known as the **Steel Pier**. When I was a kid this still had lots of iron work attached to it but I believe most of this has now gone. The Pier was the terminus of a railway track running down the cliff from an Ochre Mine in the field above from which ships were loaded. This I believe was an ill-conceived venture and the business failed. The mine buildings are long gone but I think when I was a kid the outline of the foundations were still there. Across the beach is a large square-ish rock on roughly the high water line known as **Pigs House Rock**. I am not sure if this name comes from its shape or from the fact that there may have been a pigs house in the fields above. Further along the rocks at the base of the cliff is a group of rocks which protrude into the sea known as **Jobbles**. Between these two in the field at the top of the cliff is an outcrop of rock known as **The Cairn**. Further along, at sea level, where the cliff turns almost at right angles is a shallow cave known as **Pabyer Hole**. Just off the cliff close to Pabyer Hole is a rock known as **Main Thomas**. Continuing along the shore line next comes **Bodrugan's Leap**. This is where, it is said, to avoid being caught by King Henry VII men (Richard Edgcumbe and William Trevanion) Sir Henry de Bodrugan rode his horse off the cliff to catch a waiting sailing ship. He escaped to Ireland but lost his vast fortune. Next comes **Turbot Point** the headland you can see from Boat Beach. Unseen from the village around Turbot Point on the other side of Colona Beach is **Chapel Point** with a number of houses on it.

Chapel Point

I suppose I should now mention the obvious. The rock in the centre of the bay is the **Gwineas**; or on some maps the **Gwingies**. When we were kids this rock was only ever referred to as **Gull Rock**. I'm not sure when Gull Rock went out of fashion but I never hear it used now. The large rock in the bay off Portscatho is also the Gull Rock and I have seen an old map on the wall at Cotehele House which shows the Gwineas as Gullrock.

The Bell Buoy

The navigational Buoy to the west of the Gwineas which we always refer to as the Bell Buoy although it now has a light on it and can be seen from the beach. It is not there, however, to guide shipping away from the Gwineas as you would imagine but to warn shipping away from a set of submerged rocks to the West and behind the Gwineas known as the **Yawl or Youll**. At low tide these rock are close to the surface and can be seen if you sail over then in a small boat.

The big rock immediately behind the quay is **Cadycrowse**. The headland to the right is as everyone knows **Pen-a-Mean Point**. The area of water between Cadycrowse and Pen-a-Maen Point is known as **The Pool.** It is a very sheltered spot always calm except when the wind is in the East or North East. Traditionally the fishermen kept their store pot here. Store Pots, as the name implies, are large crab pots in which Crabs and Lobsters were stored until the catch was large enough to take to market.

Continuing along the coastline of the Pool there is a rock known as **Schovella**. This is roughly where the outfall of the old sewer pipe is. Next is a rock with the name **Long Point**, a thin piece of rock at right angles to the cliff. Next is **Blackannie Island**. Neither black or an island but looking a bit like a mini version of the Blackhead between Pentewan and Porthpean. I assume it gets its name from the fact that Blackannies nested there - Blackannies being the local name for Black Back Gulls. Just inside Pen-a-Maen is a small cave which some know as **Pollack Net Hole.**

Around the point is a rock called **Trigwal** also known by Mevagissey men as Trigman, next come a pair of rocks known as the **Tar Barrels.** The rocks at the start of Vault beach are known as **Cadythew**. About three quarters of the way along Vault beach below low water is a sandy gap in the otherwise rocky sea bed known as **Land Lady.**

As you cross the bay towards the Dodman there are a couple of land-based features used by fishermen. There is **Middle Edge (Hedge)** that divides the clifftop fields and towards the end of the beach is **The Quarry** but known as **Proctor's Pit** by the Meva men.

Right at the end of the beach where the Dodman starts is **Penveor Cove**, sometimes called Star Cove, which I have mentioned before, and **Penveor Point**. Just off Penveor Cove and inside Penveor Point is an area of submerged rocks known as **Flat Rocks** for obvious reasons.

Off the end of the Dodman is a rock known as **Murton Rock** and half way up the cliff face on the end of the Dodman when viewed from the correct angle is a rock which looks like a **Horse's Head** and has that name. Below it on the sea bed is a sandy patch known as **Hoss Sands.**

Just off the Dodman is a stretch of water known as the **Gallese** (my attempt at spelling).

As you approach the Dodman by boat from the western, Hemmick, side I am told there are a couple of rocks on the Dodman known as **The Cocks Head** and **The Lions Head** because of their shape. As kids we did not often venture around the Dodman so these marks were not known to me.

Blue Point.

Chapter 7.

WEAPONS OF MASS DESTRUCTION

(Not quite so deadly)

As mentioned previously, in the early 1950's, we were all outdoor kids from the age of four or five being left to our own devices with very little supervision.

The game of choice for us boys was Cowboys and Indians. Not many of us had full Cowboy outfits but we all stretched to Cowboy hats and holsters with replica colt 45s. We wore the holsters strapped to our legs and practised the quick draw as seen on the TV. The guns all fired "caps", little explosive capsules which came on a roll which fitted into the gun and which went off with a loud crack when the trigger was pulled and the hammer fell. A small puff of smoke was created and sometimes a spark. We ran about the streets firing at each other. I can imagine that today this action would result in the rapid appearance of the Armed Police Unit. Those of a certain age will remember the TV series of the early 50s: The Lone Ranger with his Red Indian sidekick Tonto and his catch phrase 'Um good plan Kemo Sabe'; The Range Rider and his buddy the all American boy Dick West and the Mexican pair The Cisco Kid with his mate Pancho. These were must-see TV if you could get access to a set. There were not many in the village in the early 50s.

As well as a revolver I also had a replica Winchester Repeater rifle which had a magazine which held a roll of paper which exploded like caps when fired. I used to collect the ends of the ticket rolls discarded by bus conductors, cut them down the middle length ways to fit the magazine. This worked perfectly. This rifle was the only Christmas present I ever remember asking for. After making the request I worried for months that I had asked for more than my parents could afford and then as it got nearer to Christmas I then worried that it would not be at the bottom of the bed on Christmas morning. Obviously it was. It was bought, I think, on the never-never from J.D. Williams' catalogue, a routine way of buying things at the time.

An essential tool for a 50s boy was a pocket knife. Without one it was impossible to make a fishing line, gut a fish, cut a bow and arrows, make a whistle, carve a yacht out of a piece of cork, make a peashooter, make a catapult and much more. We also all carried sheath knives attached to our belts. I still have, and use regularly, a stainless steel Ex-Army pocket knife which I had as a kid. I also still have a scar on my thumb inflicted when this knife slipped when carving a piece of cork. Some of my friends, I think, progressed to flick knives and switch blades.

We walked miles searching hedgerows for forked sticks from which to make our catapults. The Y had to be as symmetrical as possible and of the right thickness. The elastic was a strip of discarded car inner tube obtained from Ern Liddicoat's garage with a leather shoe tongue, or something similar, as a pouch for the ammunition. Quite lethal weapons. I still have scars on both wrists because I did not hold the catapult upright when firing. We shot at everything that moved and some things that didn't but rarely hit our targets.

It wasn't long before we progressed to air guns, both pistols and rifles and some of my friends went on to own shot guns. My air rifle was bought from a school friend when I was about 12 years old. Nothing interesting in that but........ Unfortunately he brought the gun to school, the St. Austell Grammar, on the day the whole school walked from Poltair through St. Austell to St. John's Church in Bodmin Road for the annual Carol Service. What was I to do? The gun could not be left unattended in school whilst we went to the Service; there was no time for my friend to take it back home, so........I took it to church. I wrapped it in my coat and hoped. It was not discovered and after the service I brought it home on the school bus. I still have it but it has not been fired for about 20 years and I doubt that it is any longer in working order.

When I was about 12 a friend only a few years older than me bought a double barrelled 12 bore shot gun. The barrels were one above the other, not side by side, and I think it was described as up and over. It also had a cartridge magazine and a pump action. At the time I was told that there was a bounty on the heads of shags because of the fish they took and so we often went shag shooting. I rowed the boat out to the Pool behind the

Quay and my friend sat in the stern with his gun. As we approached, the shags would take off and my friend would take pot shots. This was fine until one day a shag he was aiming at decided to fly back over the boat and I found myself looking down the barrel of the gun. As I am still here you know he did not pull the trigger. It was, however, the last time I went shag shooting with him. He still lives in the village and if he reads this, will, no doubt, remember these shooting trips.

Gorran Haven from the east seen in June 1939 on a Tuck's postcard.

Chapter 8.

THE GREAT WHITE WHALE

(Notable for its smell)

As my recollections of this event are very sketchy I must have been very young and therefore assume it occurred in the very early 1950s. One morning Gorran Haven residents woke up to a very strong and unhealthy pong. On investigation it was discovered that during the night a long-dead whale had washed in to Little Perhaver and become impaled on the rocks by Johnny Pateman's Hole. I cannot remember any discernible features or whether it was whole or only part of the animal. It was a large very white rubbery mass with a smell impossible to describe.

In his book, Moby Dick, Hermin Melville writes " *the whale alongside must be what the fishermen call a blasted whale, that is, a whale that has died unmolested on the sea, and so floated an unappropriated corpse. It may well be conceived, what an unsavoury odour such a mass must exhale; worse than an Assyrian city plague, when the living are incompetent to bury the departed. So intolerable indeed is it regarded by some, that no cupidity could persuade them to moor alongside of it."*

I am not sure what time of year it was but I don't think it was during the summer holiday season. However, when word got out, this whale became a bit of a local attraction. I have pictures in my head of ant like lines of people walking, at low tide, across Little Perhaver to and from the rotting beast.

It was decided that the best way of solving the problem was to attach the corpse to a fishing boat and tow it out to sea. Unfortunately as the whale arrived at the top of a falling spring tide it was stuck fast on the rocks. All immediate attempts to move it failed. The only solution was to wait for the next full spring tide which, it was calculated, would allow its removal. During this wait it was also decided that towing the whale off the rocks would not stop it returning on a later tide so the decision was made, that once freed from the rocks, it would be blown up well out at sea. I am not sure what authority made this decision or who was employed to do the blowing up.

When the day came, at high tide, the whale was attached with long lines to two local boats. I think Frank and Monro Guy in the Valsheda and Lewis Billing in the Coral Reef were the people and boats volunteered for the job. After much pulling the whale eventually broke free and was towed out to well behind the Gwineas where it was blown up. Job well done everyone thought!!!

Unfortunately, a few days' later visitors to the beach were confronted by a shoreline littered with lots of two to three foot pieces of stinking blubber. Brought back from whence they came by the wind and tides. From the Quay it was possible to see these large white blobs scattered along the shore line on Big Perhaver all the way to Pabyer Hole.

I wonder if the same solution would have been employed today.

Chapter 9.

GORRAN PRIMARY SCHOOL

(Of School House In The Wind fame)

Gorran School before the fire of 1967.

By the time I started at Gorran School in 1950 we were living above what is now the Mermaid Café. On my first day I was walked to school by a friend of my mother who had a daughter starting on the same day. This *young* lady still lives in Gorran Haven and remains a very good friend. This day was the only time I remember being accompanied by an adult. Only a very few parents had any form of transport so being driven to school was out of the question. We walked the mile and a quarter in both directions whatever the weather. At that time if you failed the 11 plus exam you stayed at Gorran School until you left at 15. This meant that although we walked without parental supervision we were *looked after* by the older children.

The teachers at the school at that time were Mrs. Dyer, Mrs. Trudgeon and the headmaster Mr. John Teague. Mrs. Dyer, a rather large lady with ample bosoms, took the reception class and we were all very frightened of her. She shouted a lot and I can remember being hit on the head from behind with a drum stick when not chanting the alphabet loudly enough. One of her favourite punishments was to make one sit on the window sill. This does not seem too drastic but when you consider the sill was about 3 feet above the floor this felt a mile high to a 5 year old and was very frightening. The room was heated by a free standing black cast iron Tortoise coal fire which, when lit, became glowing hot and was surrounded by a metal fireguard for safety. During the Summer, when the fire was not lit, another punishment was to sit you on the top of this fire behind the fireguard. This was like being in prison.

Mrs. Trudgeon was young and, I think, newly qualified, and a very nice lady who took the seven and eight year olds. I can, however, remember one occasion when she made me stand on a desk whilst she pulled down my socks and smacked the backs of my legs with a wooden ruler. Conveniently I do not remember why.

Mr. Teague was a tall man who taught the class the years before the 11 plus was taken. He was very religious and was a lay preacher at the Zion Chapel located on the path to Fort. He was a strict disciplinarian who introduced his beliefs into every lesson but was a very good teacher. The year I took the 11 plus, I think, only one pupil failed to pass.

At that time the older children, amongst other things, did basket weaving and gardening to fill their time. Having failed the eleven plus it seemed that any additional education was considered of no value. The cane used as handles for the baskets was also used as the cane used for punishment. Caning when deemed necessary was administered by Mr. Teague in the passageway inside the front door of the old school. One was made to hold out a hand, palm up, and each stroke was applied as close to the tips of your figures, where it hurt most, as his aim would allow. With experience one could move the hand forward at the appropriate moment so that the stroke hit your wrist or even better the sleeve of your coat.

Outside of school and preaching, Mr. Teague had a rowing boat which also had a sail which he used to help his rowing if the wind was in the right direction. He kept this boat in the ground floor of the Old Life Boat house next to the Lime Kiln. I was told he had a favourite fishing mark three miles off the Dodman. He fished for many years after he retired from teaching and always managed to catch some very nice Pollack.

I can remember morning keep fit sessions. We were all ushered into the front playground, no matter what the weather, to do running on the spot, star jumps, skipping, and picking up bean bags with our bare toes. We progressed to leap frog and hand stands against the surrounding wall. There is currently a lot of talk about obese children and the lack of sports facilities. In my day there were definitely no facilities but there was also very few obese kids. We ran a lot and we did these exercises.

Unfortunately this school made famous by Anne Treneer in her book "School House In the Wind" burnt down in 1967 and was replaced by the current one.

Gorran School after the fire of January 1967.

Chapter 10.

RULES TO BE BROKEN

(Made by her indoors)

I think I mentioned in an earlier piece how the kids of the village were given the freedom to roam unsupervised provided they kept to a number of rules laid down by those in charge. It needs to be remembered that in the 50s Gorran Haven was very much smaller than it is now and everyone living there was known to each other. The Northern boundary of the village was Llawnroc, the Coastguard Station and Cliff Road. The Westerly boundary was the fields which are now the Car Park and the Southerly boundary was the bottom of Foxhole Lane and the Suez path. There were a few properties along Canton and Rice Lane and a cluster around the Triangle and that was about it. Stranger danger did not exist.

The rules mentioned previously were: No rock climbing, no boating until we could swim, the red beret to be worn at all times, and home in time for meals and bed. However, we all know that rules are meant to be broken.

The urge to climb was satisfied by Fort Point, Red Rock and over the rocks to Big Perhaver. We also climbed over the back of the quay playing along the exposed sewer pipe at low tide and over the rocks in search of shore crabs and gulls eggs. We sometimes fished from the rocks behind the corner of the quay. I also had a friend who lived in Llawnroc, at that time a private members club. The top drive, which was where the spur on Chute Lane is now, was lined with a row of large conifers, Pines I think, which were ideal for climbing. It was possible to climb the first tree to its canopy and then traverse from canopy to canopy climbing down the last tree. Part of the drive still exists as the entrance to the property, which was originally the coach house situated in a walled court yard. Just after the entrance, on the right, was a tennis court roughly where Lawn House now is.

Boating was a more difficult issue as the beach and harbour were in full view of my, and my friends', parents. Boats were like magnets and I had a friend who always had access to a rowing boat. I think they were owned by his extended family. There was the Wren, a clinker built boat, about 10 ft in length, and painted in pale blue and white and the Iris, carvel built, and slightly longer, painted in dark blue and red. So that my parents could not see what I was up to I used to climb over the back of the quay at its corner and my friend would come around and collect me from the rocks. I don't remember doing much except rowing around the pool and following the odd basking shark that occasionally came in close to the beach. I can remember an occasion when one grounded at half-tide just in front of the Pound. It flapped around until it got itself afloat and swam away again. There was another occasion I remember well when my friend put me ashore at the ladder on the end of the quay. As I reached the top I recognised the pair of feet and legs that confronted me as those of my mother. I got hammered all the way back along the quay for breaking the rules. I must have been less than 7 years old as by the time I was 8 we had moved to the Coastguard Station and my mother did not have such a good view of the harbour. I learnt to swim, initially with a rubber ring, when I was about 11 or 12, later than my friends, and then the boating rules were lifted.

Meal times were kept to by asking anyone we could find with a watch what the time was. If we missed a meal time, as well as getting punished we did not eat. Meals were therefore very important. Bed times were more of a problem, especially on light Summer evenings, as what kid wants to go to bed?. There were many times when I remember being fetched by an irate parent.

A 1940s postcard of Gorran Haven with the Coastguard Cottages and the line of pines at Llawnroc clearly visible.

Chapter 11.

GUY FAWKES NIGHT

(Always freezing cold)

I have been reminded of Guy Fawkes Night in Gorran Haven in the late 1950s when I was becoming a teenager.

It needs to be remembered that in those days there were no restrictions on who could buy fireworks so we all bought our own with our pocket money. At the same time fireworks were nothing like as sophisticated as they are today. The pretty ones that I can remember were Roman Candles, Vesuviuses, Catherine Wheels and, of course Sparklers and Rockets. The reason their names do not come to mind is that we boys were only interested in Bangers and Jumping Jacks.

I remember the firework makers of the time were Brock and also Standard Fireworks. The bangers had names like Cannon and Little Demon.

Fireworks were lit with a piece of tarred rope found outside Big Cellars where it had been discarded by a fisherman. A 6 inch length would last for ever because, after being lit, the flame was blown out and the rope would continue to smoulder indefinitely. No need to worry about wind blowing out matches or lighter flames.

Needless to say we got up to mischief a long time before the 5th of November. The technique was to light up your banger, wait until the fuse was burning steadily and then throw it at your target. There were individuals who lived in the village who were regular targets, usually school teachers. Under cover of darkness we would throw a fusillade of bangers as close to their front doors as we could and then run before we could be caught. This happened every year and we were never caught so I think the "targets" must have tolerated our little bit of retribution.

There were other less acceptable incidents such as the time a banger was thrown into the chapel porch during a service. Some of us, who could be identified, were punished for this event. A banger thrown into the public toilets also made a rather nice sound I remember and you could explode a milk bottle by dropping a banger into it.

Jumping jacks thrown into a crowd were also good for a laugh as it was impossible to tell in which direction they were going to jump and people scattered in all direction. I have not seen these on sales for many years so assume Health and Safety has won the day.

For a few years with the kind permission of the late Frank Lobb we were allowed to build a bonfire in the carpark. We collected anything combustible for weeks in advance and built what we thought at the time was a massive fire. Then on Guy Fawkes Night villagers brought their own fireworks and we all shared each other's offerings. I am ashamed to say that the remnants of the fire were never cleaned up with the same enthusiasm as it was built and could lie around for weeks.

Health and Safety had not been heard of at that time and fireworks were just stuffed into pockets. I can remember one occasion when a spark must have landed in my friends pocket and its contents all went up at the same time. I have this picture in my mind of him running backwards as if away from the danger with sparks of many colours shooting from a hole in his coat. I think eventually he worked out that the best solution was not to run but to remove his coat. I am not sure what state his clothes were in after this event but I do know he was not harmed.

Another clear memory was the cold. I remember Guy Fawkes Night as always being freezing. Must have been before Global Warming!!!!

Gorran Haven Harbour in the 1950s.

Chapter 12.

THE FLOWER SHOW

(A Favourite of my father's)

In the 1950s an annual village event was the Flower Show. This was held at The Institute in late summer, I think. There were many classes for flowers, fruit and vegetables also for cooking, needlework and children's drawings so almost anyone, could take part.

As well as prizes for each class of vegetable there was a Perpetual Challenge Cup for the person who had the maximum number of points accumulated from all of their winning entries. Anyone who knows me will also probably know that my late Father was a very keen gardener and a regular contributor to the show. He took great pride in entering as many flower and vegetable classes as he could and regularly won the Challenge Cup. His main rival for this cup was the late Archie Smith. They had many a friendly battle and I would guess that, if the Cup still exists, their names would appear most often on it.

Preparations for this show would start many weeks before it was due. For vegetables like carrots and parsnips this preparation would start even before the seed was sown. Soil was especially prepared and any stones which might prevent the root from growing straight would be removed. Sometimes the seeds were sown in dustbins or buckets.

For cabbages and cauliflowers individual plants were identified as having potential and these would be cossetted. Cabbage White butterfly eggs would be removed before caterpillars could develop. I can remember potatoes being selected ahead of the show, being wrapped in newspaper and stored in a cool dark place. I can also remember being told off when picking peas for the show because I had touched the shell by mistake. This ruined the natural smoky bloom which existed on freshly picked peas.

Runner beans were chosen for their length and uniformity.

The evening before the show I remember as being very busy, preparing and selecting all of the entries. On the morning of the show I was always 'volunteered' to carry boxes of produce from the garden to the Institute.

My mother used to enter the odd Victoria sponge or pasty and I can remember more than one occasion when I entered the children's drawing classes. I don't remember ever winning.

Judging took place before the doors were opened to the public. Entries were always judged blind so that the judges did not know the names of the entrants until after they had decided on the first second and third order. Judges were brought in from outside the village, usually winning exhibitors in bigger shows such as St. Austell. After lunch the show was opened to the public to view the entries and it was at this point that competitors found out how successful they had been.

At the end of the afternoon any exhibit which had not been removed by its owner was auctioned off to raise fund for the Institute and to go towards the costs of the next show.

In 2018 the show was revived after not being staged for several decades.

The Flower Show Cup showing wins for P Pinto in 1955, 1956 and 1957.

Pasquale Pinto, my father, who was called Frank by locals who couldn't pronounce his name.

Chapter 13.

COASTGUARDS

(Full and part timers)

A recent meeting of the Gorran History Society reminded me that I once had a link to the Coastguards. All be it a tenuous one.

In late 1952 or early 1953 when I was seven my family moved into No. 5 Coastguard Cottage and I continued to live there until 1970. At the time of our move there were, I think, only 3 remaining full time coastguards living in the terrace plus the Head Coastguard who lived in the detached house at the Southern end. Half of the terrace had been converted into council houses, hence our move there.

The Coastguards routine jobs at that time were to rescue people stranded on cliffs by the rising tide, animals that had climbed or fallen over the cliff and not been able to get back and to watch over the bay in bad weather on the lookout for vessels in distress. The Lookout was at the top of Pen-a-Maen Point from where you could see the whole bay between the Dodman and Chapel Point.

To help the Coastguards with their duties an auxiliary team was appointed from local male volunteers. My Father was one of these. In the 50s the recognised method for rescuing the crew of any vessel which found itself in trouble within reach of the shore was by Breeches Buoy. For those not familiar with this equipment, a Breeches Buoy was like a normal Lifebuoy but within it was a canvass insert with leg holes into which the person being rescued could sit, Breeches. It also had a harness attached to stop the passenger falling out. In the event of a rescue a rocket with a line attached was fired over the stricken vessel. The crew of the vessel would pull in the line to which was attached a thicker rope. This was made fast to the vessel and then by a system of blocks and tackle the Breeches Buoy was pulled by the shore crew to the vessel. A crew member would get into it and be pulled back to shore. The process being repeated until all the crew were, hopefully, safely ashore.

To ensure that all would run smoothly when needed, the Coastguard Team, including auxiliaries, would meet quarterly on the Gruda for rocket practice. At that time there was a large pole permanently in place at the bottom of the Gruda field to represent a ships mast. As small kids we always went to watch the rocket being fired and the Breeches Buoy being deployed. I can remember one occasion when the practise took place over the harbour. The rocket was fired from the field above what is now the Cliff Path Café to the end of the quay which represented the stricken vessel. The rope was made fast to the bollard on the end of the quay and the Breeches Buoy was pulled over from the cliff top and back with the rescued sailor. I cannot remember who the brave person was who represented the sailor.

In front of the Coastguard station was a tall flag pole on which a cone was hoisted daily. I believe the way the cone was hung indicated the wind direction to those who could see it. In an emergency a maroon was fired from below this pole. The resulting explosion would alert everyone in the village. The auxiliaries would rush to the muster point. Most of the life-saving equipment was stored in the small garage-like building at Menagwins just along from Highclere. The equipment was, I believe, transported to the scene of the rescue by tractor and trailer. There weren't many other vehicles in the village in the 50s.

I can remember my Father talking about one would-be rescue when a large fishing boat went aground one night on Big Perhaver beach. How it managed this was a mystery as it was a calm moonlit night. The equipment was fetched and transported to the end of Cliff Road by tractor. From there it was carried across the fields by the coastguard crew to a position at the cliff top with a view down to the boat. Some of this equipment was search lights and large heavy batteries to power then. I can remember father saying that all the time they were struggling to carry this heavy gear they knew they were wasting their time because the batteries were never kept fully charged. As expected, the search lights did not work. From the cliff top they could see, in the moonlight, the crew moving about so they shouted down offering assistance. No one from the boat ever responded and as there appeared to be no immediate danger the coastguard team just watched and waited. After about 6 hours and as it was getting daylight the tide came in far enough for the boat to re-float and it sailed away. I don't think the boat was ever identified although there was a suspicion that it was a French trawler.

Another piece of useless information I remember was that one of the full time coastguard wives was a Mrs Williams. Mrs Williams claim to fame was that she was the person called out, day or night, in the event of a death in the village. She was apparently an expert at "laying out" the unfortunate person and preparing them for burial. I believe in those days every village had one such person.

Left to Right: Jake Liddicoat, Charlie Billing, Maurice Patten, his Father Boxer Patten, Fred Liddicoat, Francis Guy, Tommy Guy, Jacob Billing and Ern Liddicoat.

Chapter 14.

THE INSTITUTE

(Now The Memorial Village Hall)

In the late 50s and early 60s the Institute was a thriving concern and I, with another teenage friend, was on the committee. As well as annual events like the Flower Show the Institute also held daily events, especially in the winter.

On Monday evenings it used to run a Tombola night. This was before the rise of Bingo. Prizes for lines and full houses were only a few pence but it was a popular evening event and made a little money towards the Institutes upkeep.

On Tuesday evenings there was a youth club. I remember playing table tennis on a collapsible table. I cannot remember which other games we had but I do remember being there in 1963 and hearing the news of J. F. Kennedy's assassination.

On Thursdays there was dancing to records. I guess these days it would be called a Disco. Mostly Old Time which brought out quite a few of the older ladies of the village and we learnt to dance the Gay Gordons, Valeta, Military Two Step as well as the Waltz, Foxtrot and my favourite the Quickstep. We certainly knew how to party in those days!!!! I remember my favourite Quickstep music was The Twelfth Street Rag played by Peewee Hunt and his band. I don't think I could do any of these dances now. In the early 60s some of the local lads of the village formed a group called the Were Wolves so then we had live music for a while. This did not go down well with everyone and I can remember Mrs Betty Couch who lived in Sea View, just below the Institute, regularly complaining about the noise. I also remember the young ladies of the village sitting on one side of the hall, the young men opposite. It was a time when skirts were getting shorter and I can still see the ladies tugging at their hems in a vain attempt at covering their knees. A useless act as the skirts would slide back up as soon as the hem was released.

On Fridays there was a Whist Drive. There was a period when Whist Drives were very popular and every village had one. At Christmas they were quite big affairs. Each village held their event on a different night so that people could go to all of them if they wished. Normal weekly prizes for coming first was 20 cigarettes but at Christmas there were several prizes including Turkeys, joints of meat, beer, etc. I can still picture sitting opposite Miriam Billing with a cigarette in her mouth staring at her cards through a haze of smoke. The cigarette was never removed from her mouth and so the ash got longer and longer until it dropped into her lap. Occasionally she would dig into her handbag, which was always on her knee, and then, without saying a word, place in front of you, a Fox's glacier mint.

Whilst times have changed, it is good to see the Institute is still thriving these many years later. We often attend the special events they put on and we still enjoy visiting monthly to partake of their Lunch at the Village Hall. It is a pity that more people don't take advantage of this facility. It is a great way of catching up with old friends as well as enjoying a really good lunch.

Chapter 15.

POOCH'S FIELD

(A favourite location for camp building)

In the mid-50s the father of one of my friends bought the field bordering Lamledra Hill. It became known to us as Pooch's Field and for a while we regularly played there.

At the top of this field there is an overgrown quarry. It was overgrown in the 50s, full of blackthorn, elder and brambles, amongst other things. This was an ideal place for building camps, which we duly did. We could hide there from the *powers that be* and smoke our cigarettes (usually tipped Woodbines as these were the cheapest) light fires or whatever without any fear of being caught.

One of the things I clearly remember doing in this field was sledging. My friend's father had made him a sledge with each runner covered with half a car bumper. From an old Morris Minor, I think. As the field is very steep the run down it was amazing with the stop at the bottom being quite problematical. The hedge was always there as a last resort. The downside was, however, that this sledge was extremely heavy and the pull back to the top for the next run was not so exciting. Another field I remember sledging down was the one at the back of Slips. Derby's I think it's called. The winters must have been much colder then than they are now as snow was not that unusual.

Another thing I remember doing in Pooch's field was lying in the sun with a group of friends listening to records. One of the young ladies of the village had a portable gramophone. From memory this was like a small blue suitcase with a handle on the side with which to wind up the motor which powered the turntable. As the clockwork motor ran down the record went slower and the sound became distorted resulting in frantic winding to restore power. One of the records I remember listening to was Perry Como's double sided hit with Magic Moments on one side and Catch a Falling Star on the other. I think this came out in 1957 the year of my 12th birthday. Funny what little things stick in one's memory. The simple pleasures of childhood!

Chapter 16.

SAD TIMES

(Death in the Village)

I thought long and hard before writing this memory but as Gorran Haven was, and still is to some extent, a fishing village, I have gone ahead. I hope I will not upset any of the family members still living in the village. It involves the mysterious deaths at sea of Maurice Hurrell and John Ball.

Maurice had, I believe, been a full time gardener at Llawnroc when it was a private residence but had retired and lived with his wife Gertie in Glen Moor at the end of Rattle Street. In his younger days he had been a keen cricketer playing for Gorran and also for the Cornish Choughs. When I was a kid I used to deliver veg from my father's garden to Gertie each Saturday morning. This was one house call, of several I made each Saturday, which I looked forward to as I was always given a sweet and threepence for my trouble. Maurice had a small glass fibre boat which he used for pleasure fishing, usually Pollack or Bass for his own consumption.

John was a retired mason, I think. He lived with his wife Olive (formerly Olive Oliver of Rice Farm) in Schovella which is just above Little Perhaver and has a fantastic view of the harbour.

As far as I know, these two men had never been to sea together before but for some unexplained reason decided on October 21st 1964, a calm, balmy day, to go on a fishing trip. Unfortunately neither returned from this expedition.

I think I remember coming home from work to find the top of the Quay lined with people all looking seaward. Obviously when they had not returned by the time expected the alarm had been raised and a search instigated. Eventually the upturned boat was found floating inside the Dodman. John's body was found floating nearby. Unfortunately Maurice was not found until a week later.

Obviously some unforeseen accident happened but as there were no witnesses what took place can only be a matter of speculation. Anyone who remembers the extracts from Grandfather Saunders pocket book will know these were not the only fishermen from the village to have died at sea. It also goes to show how precarious a pastime fishing is, even for those who have years of experience.

What follows is an extract from K.J. Grose's History of the Pomery Family that records the unfortunate deaths of two other Gorran Haven fishermen.

"**Robert Nicholls Pomery**, as already mentioned, was a mariner. By 1858, at the age of 29 years, he had qualified as a mate (Certificate of Competency, Liverpool) and a year later as a master. He served in the 141 ton brig "Borland" as mate in 1858-59 in the Brazilian and River Plate trade and as master in 1859-61 in the West Indies trade. From 1861-63 he was master in the same ship trading in the Mediterranean, Black Sea, Adriatic and around Spain and the Azores. This ship was lost on the

19th September 1863. Robert then took command of the "Wallace" in the Mediterranean but this ship was also lost in 1864.

Having survived two shipwrecks in two years his wife Eliza apparently persuaded him to give up the deep sea as being too dangerous and return home to fishing. This he did and in the 1871 census Robert is recorded as a fisherman. However disaster was to follow some four years later when he was 45 years old. Robert was nearly drowned in a boating accident off Gorran Haven which was recorded thus:- *"21st May 1895, Robert Pomery and David Patten's boat filled and sank at Carrethew, they was pict up by James and Tom Billing- Almost drowned"* David was then 27 years old. Five years later worse was to follow when on the 3rd February 1880 Robert went out from Gorran Haven fishing with his 16 year old son Robert Henry and neither were ever seen again. *"Only two bottom boards of the boat were ever found and no bodies were washed ashore.* "

Chapter 17.

DICK PILL BOATS

(A renowned boat builder of his day)

Back in April 2016, whilst sitting in the sun outside the Mermaid Café enjoying a cup of tea, I was introduced to a gentleman asking about Dick Pill built crabbers. I could not find out what his specific interest was but he came from Falmouth. He also had with him a copy of a hand written contract between Dick Pill and William Henry Billing which he gave to me. I have mentioned Dick Pill and his boat yard, which was where the Chippy and Beach Comber now stand. I therefore thought readers might like to read the contract, so here goes. It is dated 10th October 1910.

"*I Richard Pill boat builder of Gorran Haven in the County of Cornwall do hereby agree with Mr William Henry Billing of Gorran Haven Cornwall to build a boat for him by the early part of July 1911.*

The said boat to be of the following Dimensions and Specifications.

Dimensions.
Extreme Length 23ft overall
Broadest Beam 6ft 8 ins
Depth Midships 2ft 8 ins

Specifications
Elm Keel
Oak stem and stern post. Oak frame
Keel plate, 2 Bars? And mast.

The said boat to be build for the sum of £26. 0. 0. All iron work tarring and painting to be provided by the said William H. Billing.

Terms of Payment.
£2.0.0 when the agreement is delivered and signed.
£10.0.0 when the Keel is laid down.
£5.0.0. when framed out and the remainder when completed and handed over to the owner the said William Henry Billing.
Signed Richard Pill

I do hereby agree to the above
Signed, William Billing.

Since signing the above the said William Billing has altered the length of said boat to 26ft overall at a cost of £36.0.0. and all iron work to be provided by the said owner.
Signed, William Billing."

On the document there are three postage stamps which have been written across. One states: "*By Cash............. framed out Feb 25th 11*" another states "*By cash £7.0.0. Feb ... 11 on Keel being laid*". The third stamp is by the side of the contract amendment. I can decipher "*By Cash and ....th 10*" but no more. I assume this was a payment at the time the amendment to increase the length was agreed.

Chapter 18.

GORRAN HAVEN CRABBERS

(A couple of boats not built by Dick Pill)

In an earlier piece on fishing I mentioned two boats; the Lindy Lou, owned by Fred and Jim Liddicoat who lived with Jim's wife Dorrie in Rattle Street and the Velsheda owned by Frank and Monro Guy. In the 50s Frank lived in Foxhole Lane and Munro in Elmsdale opposite the car park entrance. Both boats were built by Percy Mitchell in Portmellon, the Lindy Lou in 1952 and the Velsheda in 1954. I have recently been given updated information on these boats and so thought readers may be interested.

A friend, who lived in Penlee opposite the car park, and with whom I grew up in the 1950s and 60s has recently moved back to Cornwall to live. He owned the Lindy Lou in the early 1970s after Fred had died and Jim had retired. Jim's wife Dorrie was a great fan of Paul Robeson and she chose the name Lindy Lou from one of his songs. My friend heard that the boat was now for sale and in a boat yard in Penryn. On a nostalgia trip he went to see her.

Unfortunately she was no longer there but he was told that as she had not been sold the owner had taken her back. The yard gave him the owner's phone number. He phoned this gentleman and discovered that he was a Dorset farmer and that the Lindy Lou was on a mooring in Poole Harbour. Even more surprisingly the owner told him that he also owned the Velsheda and that the two boats were moored alongside each other.

There is something rather nice to think that two boats which for years were moored side by side in Gorran Haven, are still together, albeit, in Poole, a long way from home.

I believe open boats like the Lindy Lou and the Velsheda built by Percy Mitchell, mainly for fishing for crab and lobster, were known as Toshers.

I passed this information on to one of Monro's daughters who advised me that when Frank and Monro ordered the boat no documents changed hands. They just asked Percy Mitchell to build them a boat of about 18ft in length. Neither man went to see the boat whilst she was under construction and they waited to be told when she was ready to collect. Apparently the Britt engine which was put into the boat had been delivered before she was ready to take it and had to be kept in store for some time. Monro always blamed this delay for the engine burning oil and never working that well. Frank and Monro took the name Velsheda from a J Class Yacht which was built in 1933, for the co-founder of Woolworths, W. L. Stephenson. He named his yacht after his daughters **Ve**lma, **She**ila and **Da**phne.

The J Class boats were the Formula 1 of the yacht racing world. Only ten of them were built, all owned by wealthy industrialists of the time. As they were very expensive to build, at the cutting edge of the technology of the time, only extremely wealthy people could afford one. All but one was built specifically to compete in the Americas Cup, ironically, it was the Velsheda that was not. Some replica J Class yachts have been built more recently and J Class races are still held. For those who are interested there was a full page article about these boats in the Daily Telegraph of Saturday 20th May 2018.

Chapter 19.

THE MILDRED

(Another Dick Pill Boat)

A friend I used to work with, Clive Davies, recently posted on Facebook some really nice photos of a boat his family had owned in the mid 1960s. He mentioned that she had been built in Gorran Haven. I have obtained from him more information which I think might interest readers. She is called Mildred.

Mildred was built by Dick Pill in 1912/13 for a Willie Johns of Flushing and was named after his wife. She was an open boat, 28 feet long, had a 9 foot beam and a 6 foot draft. Her mast stood 31 feet from the deck which was added later. She was originally built for Mackerel fishing and Pilchard driving. Legend has it that the day she was launched there was a gale blowing and she got stuck between two buildings, presumably the Lime Kiln and the cottages opposite. When Clive owned her she was used for Oyster fishing on the Fal during the Winter and for cruising and racing in the Summer. Clive's family bought her from a Truro butcher named Russell Myners. (coincidentally the man working at the desk next to Clive in John Keay House was called Russell Miners)

Over the years she has had many owners. Clive's family sold her to a Truro solicitor, David Stonehouse, who painted her white, her original colour. At some point she was decked out and made into a yacht.

Another owner was the author Howard Spring who lived in Mylor and kept her there. I'm told she was mentioned in some of his books.

Alex Bailey, also of Mylor, was another owner. He cruised in her single-handed although he did have her fitted with a Stuart Turner engine. Unfortunately she went aground below Wembury Point and was holed when Alex aged 49, and sailing alone, had a heart attack and died.

According to Clive, her current owner is David Cockwell who runs the Tregatreath Boat Yard at Mylor Bridge. The Mildred has been fully refurbished and regularly appears in the Falmouth Classic Regattas.

Apparently Dick Pill built a number of Quay Boats used at Falmouth to service ships in the bay, delivering pilots etc. One of these, the Muriel, has also recently passed the 100 year mark. Pill boats, as demonstrated by Mildred and Muriel and those still in Gorran Haven, were built to last.

Another link Clive had with Gorran Haven was that in the 60s and 70s his Uncle, Aubrey Wright, lived there with his wife Sheila and their three children. They lived in the original "Blue Point" on Cliff Road. Anyone living in Gorran Haven then, will, no doubt, remember them. Sadly, neither Aubrey, nor Sheila, is with us any longer. When Aubrey needed his new Morris 1800 serviced at the White Hart Garage then off East Hill in St. Austell I used to take it in for him. I worked in nearby High Cross St. at the time. For someone who normally drove a 1957 850cc Split Screen Morris Minor this was a real treat. For a while Aubrey owned the Valsheda mentioned in the previous chapter.

Ironically when I worked with Clive I knew nothing of his link to the village.

In the article about Dick Pill boats in chapter 17 I mentioned the gentleman who gave me a copy of his contract with Henry Billing. He also gave me the outline plan of a Dick Pill boat. Just recently I had another look at this plan. Guess what? It was the plans for the Mildred! Small world hey!

Transferring a Dick Pill creation from the boatyard to the water.

Chapter 20.

WHEELS

(On various Vehicles)

I think everyone has a fascination in one way or another with wheels. I presume this starts in the pram or pushchair.

In my case my earliest memories start with toys, cars etc. I specifically remember owning, as an 8/9 year old, a US Army Jeep which was attached to bicycle brake type cable on the end of which was a rotating handle and a plunger. By winding the handle it propelled the wheels and by pressing the plunger the Jeep could be steered. I clearly remember chasing around the living room furniture behind this jeep. Before this, when I lived in "Bethel" next to the church, I remember my friends tricycle. I was 5/6 years old and my friend who lived opposite was a couple of years older. He sat on the tricycle and pedalled and I stood on the rear axle holding his shoulders. We set out in the Street by the church. We sped down the hill swinging onto the beach at the bottom to use the sand as a brake. Exhilarating but probably quite dangerous in today's world.

By the age of 10/11 we moved on to roller skates and Dillies. The roller skates of the time, c 1955, had metal wheels attached to a metal plate which was fixed to your shoes by leather straps. These were quite useless and very dangerous as any small stone on the road would stop the skate dead and propel you forward face down onto the road, skinning hands and knees. In spite of this we rode them down the Street like we did the tricycle. For the record I learnt to roller skate in the cloisters of the Certosa Di Padula in Southern Italy. My Father was brought up there. The Certosa is a disused monastery which was then overseen by my Father's family and still is. It is now a tourist attraction. Anyone interested can look it up on line by Googling - Certosa di Padula - it is possible to learn more about this old and interesting building. It is a very interesting building with a long history. I also remember my Italian cousins taught me how to tie my neck tie in a Windsor Knot on the same holiday visit in 1957 aged 12.

Now to Dillies, which, I think, have different names around the country. I remember two Dillies in particular. Dillies were usually made from the wooden boxes that oranges were delivered in in those days, scrounged from Cakebread's I think, wooden planks, sometimes washed up as drift wood and old pram wheels and axles. Commonly old pram wheels at the back and smaller push chair wheels at the front. A length of rope, attached each side of the front axle, was used to steer. One sat in the box, which had had the front removed, sometimes with feet on the front axle and ran down whichever hill we had pulled the Dilly up.

One Dilly I remember was made with large pram wheels at the back and bed castors on the front. A friend and I set out in tandem from half way up Lamledra Hill. Part way down one of the castors broke off, we lost control and shot across the road at the bottom straight into a 4 foot high stinging nettle patch. Not a very nice experience but memorable!!!!.

The other Dilly I remember was a deluxe version. This was built by another friend's Father. The steering rope was attached to a steering wheel, a pram wheel on a stalk with the steering rope attached to each side of it. It also had a wooden lever attached to the side of the box which could be squeezed against one wheel to act as a brake. The trip I remember most started above the triangle in Bell Hill heading along Cooks Level towards Llawnroc. Unfortunately the brake did not work and halfway along Cooks Level we drove straight into the front of a car. No damage was done to personnel or vehicles but when my friend's father heard of this event the Dilly was confiscated.

Moving on from Dillies to bicycles (also known as pushbikes or tread-iron). In those days it was traditional to be given a bike as a reward for passing the 11 Plus exam although I don't remember getting anything when I passed mine. My only bike was a gift from Bill Hammond who lived in Longships on Cliff Road. It was an old pre-war bike with straight handlebars. The brakes were operated by cable but were pulled up to the wheels like lever brakes. It had three gears and rusty wheels which rapidly wore out brake pads. It was very heavy but served its purpose. I don't remember what make it was.

My Father used to cycle to work in Gorran and Tubbs Mill and eventually progressed to a Moped. This was a 50cc. NSU Quickly, German I think. It had two gears operated by a clutch and twist grip on one end of the handlebars, with the front brake and throttle on the other. The rear brake was operated by pedalling backwards. I started work in St Austell in 1963 and by the end of that year started to use the Moped to get to work. Father had by then progressed to a Ford Thames van with a seat conversion and windows in the back. I would fill the tank with fuel before I left home each morning and by the time I got back to Gorran Highlanes on the return journey I needed to switch over to the reserve to get back to the Coastguard Station. A fuel range of about 20 miles, it was obviously not designed for any sort of real journey. From the moped I progressed to a second hand 200cc Triumph Tiger Cub and then to a 350cc Matchless. Many years later whilst going around a motor museum in the Lake District I found on display the exact same model Matchless.

In 1965 I bought my first car. A black split screen Morris Minor with an 850cc reconditioned engine and 87000 miles on the clock and first registered in 1957. I paid £125 and the registration was PEW 308. It had maroon leather upholstery and a heater!!! It leaked like a sieve and the well under the back seat swab used to fill with water. When it was full and you braked hard the water rushed out and covered the backs of the legs of anyone sitting there.

I bought PEW from a dealer in Carlyon Bay. I collected it after work one Saturday morning in February and the drive home was the first time I had driven a car alone since passing my test several months before. I was very nervous. The day was wet and a little foggy. I was driving with caution and when I got to St Ewe Turn I was overtaken by a Western National double decker bus. Oh the shame of it all!! For my 21st birthday in 1966 my Mother bought me a portable transistor radio which was designed to connect to a car radio aerial and which fitted perfectly on the parcel shelf of PEW. This radio, which I still have, though it no longer works, had a button specifically for Radio Luxemburg - the Radio 1 of the time. When I sold PEW in 1969 it had done over 125000 miles, had had the cylinders re-bored and new big ends. I wrecked the engine going around the John Williams roundabout with insufficient oil in the sump. I got £25 for it. The dealer in Penwithick offered me £20 and I persuaded him to flip a coin for an extra £5. I won. I thought I had done well as another dealer in Woodland Road, St Austell, had offered me only £12 10s.

I am sure you will agree no car means as much to you as your first.

A Morris Minor similar to mine at an auction at the National Motorcycle Museum in 2017.

Chapter 21

CLIFF ROAD

(Now largely over developed)

My first How Times Change piece was about the properties in The Street (Church Street) and was intended to show how the occupancy of each cottage had changed since the 1950s. I thought I might now do the same for Cliff Road.

My family moved into the Coastguard cottages in 1953. I was 7 years old. For some of what follows I have had to enlist the help of friends to refresh my memory and for this I thank them.

Starting at the first bungalow on the right after the top of the Street and now known as Tickety-Boo, This was owned by Jack Hennah. Jack was, I think, retired. He was a smallish man with only one eye. I have no idea how he lost the other one. He was a keen gardener and was well known for pushing, after every Easterly gale, wheel barrow loads of seaweed up Church Street to his garden, to be used as fertiliser. As mentioned earlier he took in a young man as a lodger in the 50s who became known locally, and I think affectionately, as Johnny Hopeless. This "hopeless" man was ultimately responsible for developing the withy orchard along Suez where he built three Cornish unit bungalows. I believe it was this development which led to the resurfacing of Foxhole Lane providing vehicular access from top to bottom.

The next bungalow, Schovella, was owned by John Ball and his wife. I think John worked for the builder Frank Lobb who developed Perhaver Park. I have told how John died in a mystery boating accident.

The next bungalow, Beachcliff, was occupied by Will Ball and his wife Emily. Will was, I think, John's brother. He was a very quiet man who chewed tobacco and in the 1960s allowed me to park my motor bike, and later my car, in his garden.

The next bungalow Cliff Close 2 was owned by Harry Liddicoat and his wife Lilly. He was a Carpenter and decorator. Lilly was a dressmaker.

Cliff Close 1, the next bungalow was owned by Jack Hurrell who lived there with his wife Pam and sons John and Richard. Jack ran the Lobster Pot Café which is now the Chippy and Beach Comber, and the Mermaid Cafe. The Hurrell's had a TV and I have some very happy memories of being invited to watch David Attenborough's original series on Borneo. Komodo Dragons, huge flesh eating lizards, stay in my memory.

The next property was Benvista. This was occupied by a Mr and Mrs Nicholas but was later owned by Frank Brown who used it as a holiday home. Frank's father Matt lived in Green Acres, halfway up Bell Hill. I remember Matt as an old grey haired man who drove a Ford Popular and often played snooker in the Institute. He was too old and stiff to bend over the table when taking a shot. Benvista still remains within the Brown family.

Dolphins Leap did not exist. Its site was a chicken run and vegetable garden.

The next property was Blue Point. Ther a conventional bungalow not the property it is today!!!! My brother remembers that a Mrs Richardson lived there in the 50s.

Strangely I have no recollection of her but he does and he was only 3 when we moved into Cliff Road in 1953. By the early 60s it was occupied by the Wright family who I have mentioned in previous pieces.

Caprera is the next property. Phil Pill and his wife Grace lived there. Phil was a carpenter and decorator. His workshop was Grist Mill next to the hairdressers in Canton. Phil was a direct descendant of the boat builder Dick Pill who I have mentioned many times before.

Next to Caprera was a piece of waste ground. Puffins did not exist. My father had a chance to buy this plot for £50 but, at the time, could not afford it. What might have been!!

Next came Red Rock which was occupied by a Commander Burns and his wife. Unfortunately I don't remember anything about them.

After Red Rock came Longships which was occupied by the Hammond family. Bill Hammond was I understand an engraver and jeweller who worked from home. I have mentioned him in previous articles.

There was then nothing after Longships until Perhaver House the last property on this side of the road. I am told that a Mrs Mabson lived there although I remember nothing about her.

Now to the left hand side of the road.

Unfortunately I have no memory of who lived in the two semi-detached cottages at the start of the road in the early 50s. A little later Lewis Billing and his wife moved, from his house opposite the church, into one of these properties.

Now to the Coastguard Terrace. In 1953 this was divided between the Admiralty and Cornwall Council. There were three Admiralty coastguard residences occupied by the Hull, Hall and Williams families. Then came the first Council house occupied by a Mrs Manley a widow. Next was where I lived with my parents and brother and sister. Coincidently we were neighbours of Mrs Manley earlier when we both live in the Mermaid complex at the bottom of the Street. Next came Mrs McAuliffe who lived there with three of her daughters and finally Mrs Diamond with her husband and daughter. Mrs Diamond was, if I remember correctly, a German lady. I have no idea how she came to Gorran Haven. These council properties were two up two down houses. The plumbed in bath was in the kitchen and the wooden bath cover acted as the kitchen table. The toilets were outside attached to the kitchen wall. Heating was one open coal fire in the front room. I lived there very happily from the age of 7 until I got married at almost 25.

There was no other property on this side of the road until you reached Mentone, the property opposite Blue Point. This was occupied by Henry Hunkin, his wife and daughter. Henry was a fisherman who fished from his boat Jean.

Next was Pabyer. In the 50s this was a holiday home owned by the Healey's. Mr Healey, was I believe, a director of Dunlop's the tyre and rubber company. My mother used to clean for them and I remember there was always lots of foam rubber about. Pabyer stays in my mind because it had a room in the roof which was accessed via a drop down wooded ladder/staircase. This to a 10 year old was fascinating. Mr Healey's son and wife moved into Pabyer on a permanent basis when he retired from work. Unfortunately neither is with us any longer although the property, as far as I know, remains in the family.

Next and last at that time, came Silverseas. This was occupied by the Belchamber family. Mrs Belchamber was a senior official in the local British Red Cross Society.

This road has in recent years seen many changes with new properties being erected and major alteration to many of the original buildings. The first new property to be built was the bungalow next to Silverseas. This was built by the Willis family, I would guess in the early 60's. Mrs Willis was the Head at Gorran School for a while. The first big visual change was the extension to Caprera followed by the destruction of the original Blue Point and the completely new construction which stands on the site now.

Unfortunately, whilst all of the new properties must be great to live in, with fantastic views, from an old Gorran Haven man's point of view the area has been spoilt by over development.

Chapter 22.

FOXHOLE LANE

(Before the upper floor of the chippy was made into a Flat)

Having written about The Street and Cliff Road I thought I might "do" a bit on Foxhole Lane where, in the 50s, there were very few properties with direct access onto the lane. I have to say I have relied heavily on the memories of some very good friends for this piece.

Starting at the bottom and looking up the hill the first of a block of four cottages on the left was occupied by Les and Betty Couch and their daughter Barbara. Les was a 'council man'. In those days every parish had a resident 'council man' who cut the hedges, cleaned the streets etc. Les was the man for Gorran parish. He got about on an old motor bike which, it seemed, never travelled above 20 miles an hour. I remember he had a vegetable garden at Rice directly opposite the bottom of Lamledra Hill. One special memory I have of Les was when he came to have a look around my Father's garden at the coastguards. My

Father used to grow garlic at a time when this was considered quite exotic. Anyway, Les had never heard of garlic and before anyone noticed he ate a whole raw clove. I leave you to imagine the reaction this generated from him.

Behind the Couch's was a semi-detached, one up one down cottage occupied by Mr. and Mrs. Tommy Liddicoat. This has recently been enlarged.

Next to the Couch's going up the hill lived a lady we all knew as Granny Whetter. Her name was Ada and she was the mother of Ken (more of him later) and the Grandmother of my friends. The house was The Gables.

Behind Gran lived Arthur and Iris Billing and their son and daughter.

In the next property, Ivy Cottage, lived Phil Liddicoat and his wife Betty and their children. Phil was the son of Jake and Carrie Liddicoat who lived in the three storey cottage opposite the church in The Street. He had a motor bike and sidecar and worked in the Portmellon boat builders.

The next cottage was occupied by the Whetters; Ken (Granny's son) and Beryl and their four children. I grew up with the Whetter children and was best man at the eldest son Leslie's wedding. We both went on to work for ECLP and Les took up their offer to work for them in Australia where he lived with his wife and two sons and grandchildren. Ken also worked for ECLP in later years together with my Father but I remember him driving a smallish lorry which, amongst other things, was used to take the fishmen's catch to St Austell to catch the train to market. I think this was in the 50s. This was the last property on the left. Above this point Foxhole Lane was little more than an overgrown footpath.

On the right-hand side the first two properties were the semi-detached houses opposite the Whetter's. The first was occupied by Frank and Ruby Guy and their daughter Glenys. Frank has been mentioned before. He was a fisherman working with his brother Munro from their boat the Valsheda. I remember Ruby working in the Mermaid café during the summer months.

In the adjoining property, Hillside, lived Ern Coombe and his sister called Florence.

Above this property was the back entrance to Pengarth, the first bungalow along the Suez path which I have mentioned previously.

Above these properties was a small bungalow which has recently had a second storey added. Isabel Stevens lived here. Isabel, a spinster lady, played the organ at the Methodist Chapel near the car park and was involved with the Sunday afternoon Sunday School when I went there. She also organised the annual Sunday School outings. Major events in those days for kids, and some parents, who rarely got further out of the village than St. Austell. I can remember trips to Bude, Looe and Newquay and also the coach stopping in Liskeard for fish and chips. Ironic that, coming from Gorran Haven, the places I remember visiting were beach resorts. Isabel always had a little dog, Jack Russells, I think, and also took lots of photos around the village. Some of these are included in The Institute's annual display of old village photos.

The next and last property in the lane in the 50s was the imposing Treveague house. This was owned by a Mr. Lanyion and Beattie Liddicoat was the housekeeper there. Beattie was the sister of Edwin and Alf who readers will remember farmed in the village and delivered milk door to door. Edwin lived in Step Cottage in the street and Alf in Pebble Brook in Rice Lane. When Mr Lanyion died he left Treveague to Beattie to live in for the rest of her life.

Of the 10 properties which existed in the 50s only 2, I think, are now permanently occupied following the trend in the rest of the old village.

In the 50s the two bungalows between Isobel's and Treveague did not exist and Quilver Close had still to be developed.

Chapter 23.

HOMEMADE TOYS

(Simple pleasures of childhood)

In the chapter on weapons of mass destruction I mentioned that in the 50s every self-respecting country boy carried a knife of some sort. We got a great deal of pleasure out of making our own toys so I thought I would record in a bit more detail some of the things we made. I am sure by today's standards they are all pretty naive but may bring back memories to some of you.

Sailing Boats. In the 50s the fishermen bought bails of cork which they used for buoys on nets and crab pot lines. This cork was in the form of flat irregular sheets about an inch thick. We used to pinch a piece and shape it into a flat bottomed boat. We cut a slit in the base into which we jammed a small piece of slate, found on the beach, to act as a keel. We made a hole in the top into which we jammed a length of withy, to act as a mast. On the mast we threaded a piece of newspaper to act as a square sail and off we went.

Cotton Reel Tractors. In those days cotton reels were made out of wood. We collected empty ones and made what we called tractors or tanks. A small nail was driven half way into the reel at one end. An elastic band was hooked over the nail and threaded through the hole in the reel. At the other end the band was fed through either a button, which had had the centre broken out of it, or a disc of wax cut from the base of a candle. A spent match was then fed through the elastic band and wound up to create tension. When carefully placed on the ground the band would unwind and propel the reel forward. If you over wound it, it would jump about, so judgement was needed to get the tension just right. Sometimes we cut notches in the rim of the reel to create more traction.

Matchstick Guns. For this we needed a length of elder branch, very straight and about three quarters to one inch in diameter and a metal springy stay from an old ladies corset. Strange as it now seems these were readily available when I was a young kid. Possible this was the time when this type of garment was going out of fashion. Anyway the elder branch was split lengthways to about one inch from the end and the top half removed. The pith in the centre of the branch was scraped out to leave a channel running along its length. This was why it had to be elder as it has a pithy centre. The corset stay was jammed into the end which had been left intact. It was then bent double and the loose end put into a notch which had been cut into the side. A match was dropped into the channel. The end of the corset stay in the notch was then pressed sideways to release it and as it sprung forward it shot the match out the front end. Unfortunately not very far or very accurately.

Whistles. A piece of sycamore was needed for this, preferably in the spring when the growth was young and sappy. About an inch in diameter and about two inches long was ideal. A diagonal slice was taken off one end to create a mouth piece. The surface of the wood was then gently tapped all over to make the sap rise. When ready by carefully twisting the bark it could be removed in one piece. I don't think this would work with other types of wood. The inner wood then had a notch cut into it about an inch in from the end and a sliver of wood was taken off the top from the notch to the end. The bark was then replaced and a hole cut in it above the area that had been removed from the wood below. Whistle made !!!! I am embarrassed to same that, although I made many of these as a kid, one I tried a few years ago was only partially successful.

Pea-Shooters. All that was needed was a length of bamboo nicked from somebodies garden, the thicker the bamboo the better. Llawnroc was always a good source. The bit required was cut from between the notches in the cane. Pea-shooters were mostly in use when Ivy was in full berry as this made perfect ammo. You filled your mouth with berries and fire at anyone within range. I am proud to say I was quite a good shot.

Pen Nib Darts. When we got into Mr. Teague's class at Gorran School, aged 8 or 9, we were taught to write with dip pens. Each desk had its own inkwell. The nibs were replaceable so there was always a supply about. By jamming the back end of the nib in a door it was possible to split it half way along its length. Then by breaking out the pointy bit at the other end you could create two points at either side of the nib. Then using a clever bit of origami you could fold a piece of paper into the shape of a flight.

This was then slotted into the slit you had created at the back of the nib. This little dart could then be thrown at anything that had a softish surface. It would stick nicely into a door for instance.

I have previously mentioned Catapults, bows and arrows and dillies. All of these, plus the above, involved the use of knives in their construction. You can see why they were an essential piece of every young boy's equipment.

Gorran Haven in June 1939 in a Tuck's postcard with the Coastguard Station on the top left.

Chapter 24.

HONEY BEES

(But not so Sweet)

In a previous chapter I mentioned the allotments at Parc-en-Gates. This memory relates to a bee hive removed from these allotments.

In the early 1930's my father, in his early teens, lived in an orphanage, run by his uncle, in a disused monastery, close to the hilltop village of Padula in Southern Italy. He told us that, at this time, he kept bees in the alcoves in the monastery walls.

Jump forward about 20 years to the mid-1950s and he found himself living at 5 Coastguard Cottages, Gorran Haven with a wife and three children under 10. The four end cottages had been empty for a long time and the gardens were very overgrown. Each cottage had a back garden the width of the cottage, about 15ft, which was very long. When combined, these gardens covered the area now occupied by the old peoples bungalows off Chute Lane. Father cultivated his strip but it was too much for the ladies who lived on either side of us and so he also cultivated some of their gardens. Over the boundary towards Parc-en-Gates were the allotments. On one of these allotments was a beehive. The allotment and hive were abandoned and eventually someone suggested that my father take on the Bees. Somehow he got the hive over the adjoining hedge and positioned it at the top of his garden strip. Eventually the day came when he decided to check the hive for honey. My brother, sister and I were stationed in the garden shed, out of harm's way but where we were able to watch proceedings. Father decked out in hat and protective net and gloves, attempted to open the hive. All hell broke loose. The swarm, which had not been handled for many years, attacked him en masse. He had no option but to make a run for it. I can picture him now jumping into the undergrowth a couple of times on the way back to the cottage to try to shake the bees off. They continued to follow.

My brother, sister and I were marooned in the shed for what seemed like days but I think was about 3 hours. During this time father appeared several times in the distance shouting to us to stay where we were. As it began to get dark the bees settled and we sneaked back to the safety of the house.

My mother always said that the bees which got into the house, when killed, filled a "sifter". (For the non-Cornish a "Sifter" is a shovel used for adding coal to, and removing ash from, an open fire). My father's face, neck, hands and arms were covered in bee stings. I cannot remember the total number of stings but I believe there were at least 12 in his top lip alone. His face was very swollen for several days, especially around his eyes and obviously his mouth.

After this incident the bees were deemed to be too dangerous to keep and were gassed and the honey recovered. The hive was full and it was only the honey which stopped it falling apart. Father never kept bees again!!

Jump forward another 20 years to the mid-70s and my father was living in a split level bungalow he had built on a plot in Perhaver Park adjacent to the Coastguard Cottage garden. He called it "Alba". Jump forward another 20 years or so and for family reasons the bungalow had to be sold. We emptied it of its contents. In the cellar below the garage, we found several earthenware jars full of 45 year old honey!!!!!!!.

Incidentally, the monastery at Padula is now a tourist attraction and is still managed by members of the Pinto family.

Certosa di Padula
(Photo courtesy of the Italian Ministry of Culture and Latitudes Travel Magazine)

Chapter 25.

THE LIME KILN

(The age old meeting place)

For as long as I can remember the Lime Kiln was open to the public and in the 1950s was a regular meeting place for locals. In an age before mobile phones and when hardly anybody had a land line, communication between friends was not that easy. Texting had not been invented. If you wanted to meet you either had to physically knock on a door or you could "go down Lime Kiln ". If you did this you would almost certainly meet one of your mates who were hanging about waiting for someone to turn up.

The fishermen when not at sea or not making pots, repairing nets, etc. would gather on the Lime Kiln to put the World to rights. They could frequently be found walking to and fro, parallel with the front wall, crossing in the middle, and the tobacco chewers among them would spit as they turned at the end. I have mentioned before how I used to go there just to listen to Charlie Billing talking.

In those days the surface of the Lime Kiln was made up of what was basically hard-core. It sloped from the front wall down to the present road level. In the centre was a large circle of red bricks set into the surface. I believe this was, before it was filled in, the top of the kiln into which limestone blocks were loaded to be fired and turned into lime to be used by local builders and farmers, etc.

As well as a meeting place we kids played football there, rode our bikes there and as we got older it was an ideal vantage point in the Summer for identifying talent (young ladies) on the beach.

In the 50s there were no seats on the Lime Kiln and during the Summer it was used as a car park. The cars were packed in, parked bumper to bumper under the guidance of "the parking attendant" Jacob Billing. Jacob lived with Mr Francis and Mrs Julia Lafitte in the basement of the Customs House next to Cakebreads called Sea Way. Julia was Charlie Billings sister so I assume Jacob was also a relative. Jacobs instructions were not that clear and there was a standing joke that would go, "back,

back, back" CRASH " Wow!" I can remember at least one lady holiday maker who had both legs crushed by a car, I think on the Lime Kiln, although I don't think Jacob had any hand in that incident. Jacob was in possession of a loud hailer through which he shouted out car numbers from the Lime Kiln wall when he needed someone to move so that a car parked at the back could be let out.

The building currently in use as the Doctors surgery was used by the fishermen as a place where they accumulated their catches ready for collection. Ken Whetter with his small lorry was used to transport the catch to St Austell where it was put on a train for, I believe, the London market.

The Lime Kiln is still a meeting place and a sort of focal point in the village thanks to the generosity of Tommy Billing. He gave it to the Parish Council so that it could be kept open to the public. Long may this continue.

Chapter 26

THE GOOD OLD DAYS

(or maybe not so good)

During the first lockdown in April or May 2020 I caught myself referring to "the good old days". This set me thinking about whether they were really that "good". In 1953 a few months before my 8th birthday my family moved into one of the four Coastguard cottages then taken over by the Council and offered as council houses. 1953 seemed therefore to be a good time to compare with today. I also thought it would show what life was like for a young lad back then, at least one living in Gorran Haven. I think my life was no different from many of the people who lived in the old village then. I am sure older readers will have similar memories and young readers might also find it interesting. I hope so anyway.

I have listed, in no particular order, a few of the things that everyone has now but which we lived without in 1953.

Cars: We didn't have one and neither did most of the families living in the old village at that time. My Father used to cycle to work as a farm labourer. He bought his first vehicle in 1957 or 1958 when he was close to 40. It was a second hand, pale blue, Ford Thames van that had a kit conversion. It had had windows and a set of seats fitted in the back. The seats could be folded down to create space for carrying larger items. A sort of early three door hatch back. He had quite a serious accident in this with my Mother as a passenger on Pengrugla corner. I remember she was very bruised by the seat belt. I bought my first car in 1965 when I was 20. A black 1957 split screen Morris Minor with 87000 miles on the clock. It cost me £125.

TV: We got our first TV in the late 50s when I was 12 or 13. It had a 14 inch screen and was in its own floor standing wooden cabinet. I am not sure but think it was a Ferguson. The picture was black and white. It had knobs to control the horizontal and vertical holds. Occasionally the picture would slip sideways and the horizontal hold control was then employed. On other occasions the picture would roll vertically. Often the best way of stopping this was to slap the top of the set rather than employ the controls. There was no remote and only two channels to watch, BBC and ITV. BBC2 was introduced in 1964, Channel 4 in 1982 and Channel 5 in 1997. I don't think I had a coloured set until sometime in the 1970s after I had married.

Central Heating: The cottage we lived in had only 4 rooms, two up and two down. The only heating was an open coal fire in the sitting room. It was never referred to as the lounge. (This was a word reserved for use by pubs and hotels. I remember much later when Llawnroc got its licence you paid more for a pint in the Lounge bar than you did in the Public bar.) Our sitting room was about 15ft by 10ft and the fire was on the shorter wall back to back with that of next door. I will leave you to imagine the competition there was between 5 of us for the space in front of this fire.

Ensuites: I'm afraid not, not even a bathroom. The toilet was on the outside on the back wall of the cottage back to back with the one next door. Admittedly it was only a few paces from the back door but it was a journey to avoid when it was raining or the middle of a winter's night. Modern day toilet tissue, although, I think, invented in the UK, did not start to become widely available until after the Bowaters Paper Co. merged with the American company Scott Paper Co. in 1956. I don't think it reached Cornwall until much later than this. The elderly amongst us will remember the most commonly used paper of the time, branded IZAL. It came on a roll but it had the texture of grease proof paper. I think I need say no more on this subject. Runny noses were managed with square cotton handkerchief. There was nothing disposable available.

The bath was in the kitchen. It had a wooden cover hinged to the wall which also served as the kitchen table. Water was heated by an electric heater on the wall above the sink. We always ate as a family and as it was only possible to sit around two sides of the table my mother always sat behind us and ate her meals from her lap.

Washing Machines: Mother washed everything by hand as did everyone at that time. Clothes were dried on the Line when the weather was good but otherwise on a contraption in our kitchen. I don't know its name. It was a series of wooden slats on a frame fixed to the ceiling via a pulley system and which could then be raised and lowered. It was lowered so that you could drape the wet clothes over the slats and then hoisted to the ceiling to make space below. If you could afford them twin tub washing machines started to be used in the 1960s and were superseded in the 1970s by automatic front loaders. Tumble Driers were also starting to be used in the 1960s. These days hardly anything is hand washed.

Fridges and Freezers: If you felt a bit peckish you could always raid the fridge. Not possible I am afraid, we did not own a fridge and, as we were not allowed to eat between meals, it would have been banned anyway. In the 1950s perishables such as milk, butter, meat etc were kept in a "safe". Not the bank type but a wooden cupboard which had perforated zinc walls and door to allow cool air into it. This was usually fixed to an outside wall preferably in the shade. Our safe was fixed to our next door neighbour's wall in a corner that was never exposed to the sun. The ideal place. Fridges started to become popular in the 60s I believe. By the 1980s half the households in the UK had freezers. They only started to become popular when commercially frozen foods were introduced into stores.

Supermarkets: These did not exist. All grocery shopping was done locally. There were two village stores in Gorran Haven then, Cakebreads and Tubbs. Cakebreads was where it is now. Tubbs was directly opposite the Church although it later moved to the Chippy and Beachcomber site. I think this move would have been in the late 50s or early 60s. I can remember going to Cakebread's on a Saturday morning with a shopping list, a ration book and my Father's weekly pay cheque. Mr Cakebread deducted the cost of the shopping from the cheque value and gave me back the surplus. The original "cash back". Anything other than groceries involved a bus trip to St. Austell so did not happen very often. Harry Strike's in Truro Road or Phillips Outfitters at the end of Fore Street were the targets for shopping for my school uniforms. Currys, I think, for electrical goods.

Computers: Did not exist. They did not get introduced until the late 70s or early 80s. When my employer, ECLP, installed their first computer it occupied a building especially built to house it at John Keay House in front of the main block. It was still only capable of working out the company's wage bill. These days most mobile phones would have more computing power. The world wide web was not invented until the late 1980s and first became available to the public in 1993. Just shows how young the internet, that we all now rely on, is.

Telephones: There was no such thing as mobile phones. All phones involved land lines but hardly any household in the village had one. If you wanted to make a call you had to walk down to the kiosk by the toilets with a pocket full of old pennies. I can remember calls being made through an operator who, I think, was based in Mevagissey. By the 60s the kiosk had been converted to automatic. You then fed the cost of your call into a coin box, dialled your required number and when answered pressed the button to allow the coins to drop into a box beyond recovery. Some of us discovered a system to avoid paying when using these boxes. If you tapped the rest once for 1, twice for 2 etc pausing slightly between each number it was possible to 'beat the system' and talk for as long as you liked. Most phone numbers then only involved four digits so this was an easy process. Mobile phones did not arrive in the UK until the mid 80s and were then about the size of a large brick. I got my first land line in 1970 or 1971 after I had married and had moved to St Blazey.

Take Away Meals: There was no Chippy in Gorran Haven and this meant that a trip to St. Austell was a rare pleasure as it usually involved a lunch time visit to the chippy in Duke Street, always referred to as Tart Arthurs, for fish & chips, bread and butter and a cup of tea or in my case Vimto. I can remember one occasion when I was 10 or 11, so 1955ish, when I had 4 teeth removed at Probert's Dentist in South Street. After I recovered from the gas anaesthetic we then went around to Tarts for lunch. I was not going to miss the opportunity. At that time there were no foreign food outlets in the district. I doubt that many people had any idea what Italian, Indian, Chinese food was let alone Thai, Mexican, etc. I can remember the first Chinese restaurant to come to St. Austell. It was situated behind Woolworths, opposite the Odeon Cinema. The area now swallowed up by the new town centre development. My first visit must have been in the early 70s. I had no idea what anything on the menu was. Times have certainly changed.

Duvets: Although there was no central heating you could always wrap yourself snuggly into your duvet to keep warm. Sorry, no you could not! Duvets were first sold in the UK in 1964 and did not become popular until the late 1970s. You had to rely on layers of blankets and a bed spread which to this day I believe to be a more versatile system.

Ball Point Pens: In the 50s writing was a bit of a palaver. When I started school in 1950 we first started writing on a slate with a steel pointer, a bit like a nail. We progressed to pencil and paper and by 1953 had progressed to a dip pen. Each desk had an ink well into which your pen had to be dipped before attempting to write. This was problematic and blotting paper was widely used to mop up spills etc. I believe it was thought at the time that using this type of pen disciplined you to write properly! Even up to the time I left the Grammar School in 1962 ball points were banned and you were expected to write with a fountain pen. These superseded dip pens and had a rubber reservoir which held liquid ink and were refillable. For the record the Biro was first invented in 1938 and was named after its inventor. Biros were very expensive so were not widely used. The BIC was introduced in 1959 at a much more affordable price and then ball points started to be more widely used. Felt tips and the like came much later.

Fashion: We were always dressed in the height of fashion. Not true I am afraid. Fashion did not enter our vocabulary. Apart from our Sunday Best, an outfit reserved for high days and holidays, and my school uniform when I got to the Grammar School, clothes were often hand-me-downs or obtained from jumble sales which were held frequently in The Institute. I can clearly remember wearing hob nail boots. The lead seggs on the heels and toes rattling on road surfaces as you walked.

Toys: We always had plenty to play with. Unfortunately we did not. Plastic toys had not been introduced and obviously neither had computer games. Toys were made of tin plate or lead. If they were powered at all they were powered by clockwork, not batteries. I remember a present of Hornby train set which did nothing but go around and around a three foot circular track. I could never work up any great enthusiasm for it. The only games available were board games. Simple ones like Snakes and Ladders and Ludo rising to things like Scrabble, Chess, etc. Obviously there were no computers, tablets or mobile phones to play games on.

A boy in his dilly cart – unfortunately this is not me!

Chapter 27.

BOREDOM

(Saturday Morning Working)

In the late 1960's the company I worked for English Clays Lovering & Pochin (ECLP) decided that if we worked an extra 15 minutes each day we could have three out of four Saturday mornings off. This meant that the Saturday that I had to work was very boring as there was hardly anyone else in the building and none of our customers worked Saturdays. To relieve the boredom I took to writing what can, I suppose, be loosely referred to as verse. What follows are some of these which I came across recently at the back of a drawer. I thought I would inflict them on you as they relate to the village.

Gorran Haven

Quiet and serene is the harbour,
Beautiful to look at, whatever the hour.
The sea is calm and the sky is blue
No one needs have anything to do.

This is the village on a nice day
There is no place better, the locals say.
The sea to swim in, the boats to sail
Even fishermen, to tell a good tale.

In the winter, it's not so nice,
Then the wind comes, blows up in a trice,
The sea gets rough, white crests on the waves,
Pounds the cliffs, fills all the small caves.

Gulls circling and screaming overhead,
It's difficult to hear whatever is said.
Boats intentionally beached, crab pots even,
That's when the village becomes Gorran Haven.

Everything up beyond high water
Fishermen wait for the calm that comes after.
Boats will again be put to sea
The Village will once again be free.

Herring Gulls

These large grey birds glide about,
Make you jump with their noisy shout.
Dive and soar on the thermal
Enjoying themselves in the turmoil,
Clean the harbour of its offal,
All dead fish in one big swallow.

On the sea they sit for ever,
Lose their patience do they never.
Drift and paddle to and fro,
Always watching for their foe,
Human Beings, Great Black Backs
Always ready for attacks.

Gulls are everywhere on house peaks,
Dawn is notified by their shrieks.
Gulls that make the village sing,
Character to the place they bring.
Beautiful birds that soar and dive,
They make you glad to be alive.

Summer Visitors

On the beach they swarm in hundreds
Frilly sun hats on their heads.
Pulling sailing boats behind them
Waiting to get behind the helm.
Dinghies getting all the attention,
Is the wind in the right direction?

Children trailing along behind
They don't care as there's a wind.
Off with the tarpaulin covers
And their brightly coloured pullovers.
On with Life Jackets, down to the sea,
Dying to sail and be free

From the usual noise of traffic
To get the feeling that's terrific.
Off they push from the shore,
Hands and backs will soon be sore.
At the moment they never felt better
All their clothes getting wetter and wetter.

The wind behind them, what a run
On the river they get no fun.
Thousands of visitors come to Cornwall
So that they can be informal.
They don't get pushed or badgered about,
And the kids can always shout
without disturbing the neighbours.
They on their own are safe for hours.

Harbour Gala Day seen from Schovella. Photo courtesy of Geoff Fox.

Chapter 28.

PROPERTIES IN GORRAN HAVEN

(A bit of history)

"Beach House"

"Beach House (Cottage)" was, in the mid-1800s, a pub called the "Ship Inn". "Beach House" is part of the complex that contains the "Mermaid Café" and is surrounded by the sea defence wall known locally as "The Platt".

Between 1851 and 1865 the landlord was Thomas Saunders (Sanders) who brewed his own beer. Thomas Saunders, in his pocket book, records that on the 17th June 1851 he brewed 36 gallons of beer, and in the same month he paid £30 – 4s – 7d for 47 tons of coal including Freight, carriage and stowing. He also states that on the 21st January 1867 "the hend of the Ship Inn washt down".

More interestingly he also records that on the 31st January 1867 Mr. Varcoe sold the Ship Inn to Mr. W. Hicks, St Austell for £61. It is presumed that this is the

Walter Hicks who founded St Austell Brewery, I believe in the 1850s. St Austell Brewery is, of course, still going strong and I am sure many are familiar with their ales.

Thomas Saunders died on 31st January 1892 but I have no idea how old he was.

"The Chip Shop and Beachcomber"

This site was once the site of a very well-known boat builder, John PILL, 1799 – 1883, where he built working sailing boats up to 40 ft. in length. I also believe that a replica of one of these boats has recently been built in Fowey for a private owner.

The business continued in the Pill family until 1925, run by John's nephew, Richard Pill, and included an export trade. I believe his boats were well known as "Gorran Haven Crabbers" and some remain in the village and can be seen on their moorings in the summer.

"Fuchia Cottage" (next to the CHOP SHOP Hairdressers)

According to a Grose family history, researched and written by Kenneth J. Grose, this cottage was occupied by Thomas and Emma Grose for nearly all of their 54 year marriage. It then had four rooms and was built on the site of a fish cellar. Thomas was a stone mason and between June and October 1886 he worked on the building of the new quay. Thomas died at Fuchsia Cottage on 24th June 1948, aged 79 leaving a will with an estate of £233. Emma died in April 1950, aged 84 and both are buried at Gorran churchyard.

Thomas and Emma brought up two sons in Fuchsia Cottage. The elder was Robert Henry (Bob) born in 1894. He did not marry until he was over 45 years old. He originally worked as a mason but in 1935 he was left Rice Farm by his uncle and he then became a farmer. In 1940 he married Elsie Brown and went to live in Rattle Street. They had no children and he died in 1975 aged 80 years. The second son was John Wade Pill Grose who was born in October 1896. This son went to work in the post office and after serving in the First World War left the village and continued his career in the postal service until he retired in 1956. He died in Southampton in 1988 on the eve of his 92nd birthday. He was the father of Kenneth Grose the writer of their family history.

I can remember visiting Mrs. Grose as a very young child, probably preschool, as she gave us sweets and I can also remember on at least one occasion being taken by her for a picnic, to Vault Beach.

"Trelawney" (between Harbours Reach and Grist Mill)

This property was built by Susan (Susie) Pomery in about 1904 on the site of an old lime kiln which failed after the other lime kiln was built at the top of the beach. Susan was born in 1861 and never married. She was the daughter of Robert and Eliza Pomery and was one of eight children. She went to Birmingham with two of her brothers and became a Post Office supervisor. She retired following a nervous breakdown in her forties, returned to

Gorran Haven and built Trelawney. She let "apartments" there from about 1914 to 1923 and continued to live there until her death in 1946, aged 85 years. In 1880 one of her brothers, Robert, and his 16 year old son Henry disappeared whilst fishing from Gorran Haven. Neither body was ever found.

A 1940s George Ellis postcard of the harbour wall.

Chapter 29.

MY DEAR MARY nee KIRKEN

(As recorded by Grandfather Saunders)

Parish Magazine readers may remember from 2011 my extracts from Grandfather Saunders Pocket Book. At the time he wrote it he was the Landlord of the Ship Inn which was above the Mermaid Café adjoining the Platt. Recently I was asked if I had any information on the Kirken family. What follows is what I put together from Grandfather Saunders entries about his daughter Mary which I hope you may also find interesting.

Mary was born 1801. The 1881 census shows Captain Thomas Saunders (Sanders) living with his daughter Mary Kerkin (Shopkeeper) and he is listed as a naval pensioner. Mary married Samuel (Sam) Collins Kerkin on 3rd March 1863. In 1871 Samuel Kerkin was a draper in Falmouth, employing 22 female assistants and 1 male apprentice, having left Gorran for Falmouth on 10th January 1870.

Mary was, it appears, Thomas's favourite daughter as he always referred to her as My Dear Mary.

In April 1871 Thomas reports that Sam and Mary had smallpox. There is a reference in February 1872 saying that Mary was very ill. They obviously both recovered because on 23rd Sept 1872 the Kerkins came back to Gorran having handed the drapers over to a Mr Grose.

A little interesting aside. On 19 January 1869 Thomas reports that Sam's servant girl had a child in the pigs house and the child died on the 22nd. The girl, (unnamed) was charged with concealment of birth and on 18 March was sentenced to 2 months hard labour.

On the 23rd October 1872 the Kerkins sailed to Wellington New Zealand on the SS Forfarshire. They arrived on 2nd March 1873.

On 4th August 1874 a Mrs Mingo received a "wisht" letter from Mary. I believe this to be Sam's sister who married a James Mingo, the butler at Caerhays Castle. James and his wife were my maternal Great, Great, Grandparents.

On the 18th March 1875 Mary left New Zealand for London on the SS Glenlora arriving back in Gorran on 18th July. Sam came back a year later on 29th August 1876.

It would seem that the marriage had problems because on 12th June 1878 Mary left Sam with the two youngest children and went to live with Thomas. She did not stay long, going back to Sam on the 15th. On the 30th October Mary again left Sam with the two children.

On the 31st January 1881 Sam and Wallas (Wallace?) sailed to Brisbane on the SS Zamora. I assume Wallas was the eldest son as he regularly sent money to Mary.

On 11th May 1882 Wallas ship was wrecked but no lives were lost.

In 1883 Wallas went to live in a place called Mackey some 300 miles from Brisbane.

On 8th August 1883 he sent Mary £8.00 and papers for her and the children to go to Brisbane.

On 22nd October 1883 Mary sailed on the SS Merkera to Brisbane arriving on 13th December.

On 4th March 1884 there was a reference to another letter saying Montey was on a ship with Wallas. I assume Montey was another child.

On 6th September 1886 Thomas had a letter from Mary stating "she had a very bad finger, a wiklow (whitlow) on it. 2 cores worked out of it. Suffered a lot. Doctor was paid £1 for it & now they are gone 40 miles away again. Got a farm 100 & 70 ekers (Acres?) They are like a wondering sheep never stop in one place. Wallas is chief Steward in a company of steamers. Doing well & Montey is at Brisbane in the stores."

There are several references after this saying that letters had been received from Mary and all was well but there is no reference to Mary after 1886. Thomas stopped keeping regular notes after this date.

Thomas Saunders died on 31st January 1892.

Chapter 30.

OLD LOCAL FISHING WORDS

(I remember using many of these in my childhood)

Some friends and I have come up with the following list of words which we remember in regular use in the 50's and which, I think, have now largely died out in the same way as the making of withy crab pots. I hope readers find them of interest.

BILTER or BALTER: A long heavy duty line intended to catch Conger, Dogfish and the like. A larger version of a spilter.

BISHOP: A Weever fish.

BOOM: A wooden pole about 10ft long placed at 45 degrees angle from the side of a boat from the top of which the mackerel line was attached. Booms were usually used in pairs, one on each side of the boat, to keep two lines from tangling.

BOULES or BOOLs: Stones from the beach larger than a pebble often used as weights in withy crab pots.

COOK: pronounced COOOKE: A cuckoo wrasse.

CHEEM (or CHAM): Thick withies used around the outer edge/bottom of pots and which were sometimes mixed, for extra strength, with Tamarisk; a very robust wood.

CHINE: Same as CHEEM.

COCK: A male edible brown crab. Alternative to JACK however locally Jacks were male crabs about 2lb in weight and Cocks were male crabs over 3lb in weight. Somewhere in between was a crab described as a Quarter crab.

CHAD: A Sea Bream.

FID: A dictionary word for a tool used for splicing rope. Some fishermen also used this tool when making crab pots to prise withies apart to make room for an additional one. Like a large bradawl.

FORCER: An extra rib used in withy pot making to take up gaps in the ribs of the pot and which help to retain the shape of the pot.

GOOZY GAY: A small green/brown backed shore crab. These crabs were occasionally used, by the local kids, as bait for wrasse.

GAVERICK: A Spider crab.

GARLIP: A Blenny. A small rock pool fish.

HARD CHINE: Marine Plywood when used to construct a whole boat.

HUMP: A female edible brown crab. Alternative to HEN.

LANCE: A large Sand Eel.

LONG NOSE: A Garfish.

MAWN: Withy basket with handles on each side of the top used for carrying the catch, be it fish or shellfish. Each fisherman would stand between a pair of mawns and by holding a different mawn in each hand several could be carry at one time in a long row.

MEL: In the days before polypropylene, sisal was used for rope. To stop this rope getting snagged in weed or rocks on the sea bottom corks were tied onto the line about 4 feet from the first and last pots in the string and then another about 4 feet above that. These corks were Mels.

MIZZEN: A small roughly triangular shaped sail, about 4ft high, deployed at the stern of a fishing boat intended to keep the boat head to wind when hauling pots or nets.

MOTT: The mushroom shaped stump of a withy tree left after the years growth had been removed for crab pot making.

PLUMMET: A cone shaped lead weight about 3 inches high used on mackerel lines intended for towing behind a moving boat. The speed of the boat and the weight kept the line at the depth at which the mackerel were swimming on the day.

RAUNER/RAWNER: A large but very thin Pollock perhaps caught after spawning.

SKIVVER: A sharpened stick about 12 inches long and used to secure bait into the pot. A Skewer.

SNIG: A name given to a small conger eel of 2/3 feet in length.

STRAP: Same as SNIG

SPINNER: A lure for mackerel consisting of a hook with a triangular silver fin on the shank which spins when pulled through the water.

SNADE: A thin sliver of mackerel usually cut from close to the tail and added to the spinner as additional attraction.

SPILTER: A light weight line with a number of evenly spaced hooks along it length. Usually deployed from a boat, parallel with and close to the low water line, intended for catching any flat fish or bass.

SPILE: A small cork used to fill the drain hole in the bottom of the fishing boats. This was usually applied from the outside when the boat was aground so that the water pressure kept it in place.

STROP: A short length of rope which attached each crab pot to the main line.

SPRATTS: Sand Eels.

SCAD: Horse Mackerel.

SHINY FISH: A salmon or salmon peel illegal to land if caught at sea.

SPLATTY GROUND: A description for the sea bed when it is made up of a mixture of sandy patches interspersed with rocky area. Ideal for catching crab and lobster.

TRIG: A wooden wedge shaped frame placed under a boat to stop it falling on its side when aground at low water.

TICKER: A crab holed up in a crack in a rock at low water. It makes a ticking noise. Also used to describe small crabs that are just over the legal landing limit.

TRAMMEL: A pair of curtain nets. One net with small mesh and one with larger mesh. The fish were caught by swimming into the smaller mesh net and pushing it through the larger mesh to form a pocket from which they could not escape. I think.!!!

ULLY: A crab pot about 4 times the size of a normal pot with a square access door in the side secured with rope. This pot was kept in the Pool behind the quay, anchored to the bottom and was used to store crab and lobster until sufficient had been caught to make a trip to market worthwhile.

WITHY: Willow used for crab pot construction.

YAFFLE: A small bundle of withies approximately 9 inches in diameter.

A 1940s George Ellis postcard with a view from the Quay.

Chapter 31.

OTHER OLD LOCAL WORDS

(Part of what makes Cornwall Cornish)

After doing the piece on fishing words I then started putting together a list of more general dialect words which were used regularly in my childhood. Some were, I guess, specific to Gorran Haven but most I am sure were used more widely around the county. Unfortunately most of these words, or at least, their Cornish meanings/nuance are dying out in the same way as the language. It would be a pity if they died out altogether as they are part of what make's Cornwall Cornish.

Every now and then I find myself using a word that I have not used since childhood. Where in the brain they are dredged up from who knows? A few days ago I found myself using the word "shink". It came from nowhere and when I checked it was not on my list. It is now. To save you waiting for the S's it is a combination of Should and Think.

I should add that I have had many contributions from family and friends who I used extensively to jog my memory. I also discovered a list in the late Archie Smith's book "Smiles and Tears". To make my list more comprehensive and for those who have not read his book I have included his offerings. These are marked with an asterisk. I feel sure he wouldn't mind me pinching them as, after all, they were all once in common use.

Here goes:

ABROAD*: Open as in "his mouth is always abroad"; gone fat, "She's hayved abroad this past year"

AGGIBOAR: Hedgehog

ANGUISH*: Inflammation: a word which is usually said in a sympathetic tone.

ANSUM: Handsome . As in "Right me ansum"

ARAB: A cheeky child. "You little Arab"

BACK SIDE FORE: or sometimes **FORE SIDE BACK:** Inside out or the wrong way round. "You've got your jumper on back side fore"

BALLING: Crying; usually a child. "do something to stop that balling kid".

BEAUTY*: A fine example; a very attractive woman but rarely in this context. " She's a beauty", is more likely to mean that she is a bit wild and loose.

BELONG*: To belong means the place where you live. "I belong down Gorran Haven."

BILTER : A heavy duty long line usually intended to catch Conger and Dogfish. A much larger version of a spilter.

BIVERED: Shivery. "I'm bivered with the cold"

BLAKEY: Very loud or noisy

BOILING*: boiling could be very hot e.g. "I'm boiling", or swarming in numbers, "Pilchards are boiling out in the bay"

BOULES or BOOLS: Stones from the beach larger than pebbles often used as weights in withy crab pots.

BRAVISH: usually big but could be out of the ordinary.

BUDIX/BIDDIX: A garden tool like a pick axe but with a long handle and only one short wide blade used for digging. Like an Adze but much bigger. This had a large eye to take a chunky handle, hence the saying "eye like a BUDIX" for someone with sharp eyesight.

CABBY: Messy, untidy.

CACKYLATE*: To calculate: said with pride, "I cackylate that .."

CARPENTERS LOUSE: a blood blister.

CATCHPIT*: A place, in the home usually, which was used to store things in, but evokes untidiness.

CHACKS: Cheeks. " That childs got rosey chacks"

CHEELD*: Usually used instead of girl e.g. "Is it a boy or a cheeld?" when enquiring the sex of a baby.

CHIPPLE: Spring onion.

CLAGGY OR CLAGGED: Sticky or clogged.

CLICKY: Anyone who is left handed is clicky

CLOUTS: Roofing nails.

CLUCK*: Broody, "I'm looking for a cluck hen to put to sit"

CLUCKY DOWN: to squat.

COOCHY DOWN: lie down or make room for others in a small space.

COOSE: To chase but in a non- aggressive way. "I am going to coose those sheep out of my garden"

CUT UP*: this describes the speech of a dialect speaker who decides to speak English without a Cornish accent. "She's cutting up now that she's been away"

DABBY: Wilting; Plants go dabby when short of water.

DAGGING*: longing, desperately anxious. " I'm dagging to git home."

DEAR AS SAFFRON: Anything expensive.

DILLY: A homemade cart usually made with wheels from a pram and a wooden soap box, steered with a rope and which we boys used to ride down the local hills in.

DIMPSY: Half-light as in twilight**.**

DISHWASHER*: a pied wagtail.

DRANG: A small passageway or shortcut between houses.

DRECKLY: Some unspecified time in the future. When I get around to it. " I'll do that dreckly"

DRY AS CHIP: Usually food, difficult to swallow.

DRY AS CHUCK: same as Chip.

EMMETS: Ants or a derogatory word for holiday makers.

ERDERS: Apples picked specifically for storing over the winter (Horders).

EVIL*: a fork with four or five prongs which are curved.

FERRICK: To make clean and tidy. Usually a room or person.

FITCHER*: a polecat but usually used in the simile " as wild as a fitcher." – in a temper.

FITTY: A word for good, big or fit for purpose. "that withy will make a fitty bow"

FLINK*: to flick as in, "He's flinking ink," or used to describe a woman who tosses her head in a haughty or ill-tempered way.

FORERIGHT*: impulsive; at the forefront always.

FOUR-LEGGED EMMET: The common lizard. Common they were in the 50s but a rare sight now.

FRAIL or maybe FREYL: A cloth shopping bag.
FRIZZ*: The wind may be said to be frizzing if it disturbs the water's surface, also to sizzle- "that bacon is frizzing away in the pan".

GAT: Wonderment or Disbelief. The response to a statement you are surprised at.
GADDLE*: to drink frequently but not normally in large quaffs. "They two do like to sit down all morning and gaddle tea, and gossip".
GEEK: Look. "Take a geek at this".
GIDGY: A con trick or fiddle.
GONE CLUCK: Broken down. Also chicken go Cluck when past laying or sitting on a clutch of eggs.
GRAFTED*: really dirty; a person who has not washed for a long time would be grafted.
GRIZZLE*: a kind of grin, sometimes associated with a touch of impertinence.
GULLROCK: The Gwineas was always referred to, by locals, as the Gullrock.
GURT: Big or Great. "That's a gurt conger"
GUTTERS: Drains at the side of the road.

HARDHEADS: Plantains that grow in the hedgerows. They grow a stem with an oval dark brown head the size of a coffee bean. As kids we used to play a sort of conkers with then and also fired them by wrapping the stem around the head and shooting them off.

HAYVED*: spread. As in " The planks in this boat have hayved abroad over the winter.

HELLING*: the roof- "He's up on the helling seeing to the slates".

HINDERMENT*: a corruption of hinderance and widely used.

JAWING: A telling off. "She was giving her husband a good old jawing"

KISKY*: the hollow dry stem of a plant, especially hemlock.

LAMPERED: Filthy dirty as in "after playing rugby he was lampered in mud".

LATHER: beat or lash. A parent might say "if you don't stop doing that I'll lather you". A thrashing. Presumably a corruption of Leather. To beat with a belt or strap.

LAUNDERS: Guttering around a roof.

LEAK* sometime Lick: usually in the context of a little more, especially tea. "A leak more please"

LERRUPS: Rags and tatters. Also all over the place, in pieces. "Scat to lerrups".

LICKER: Anything larger than normal. "Look at that! he's a great licker".

LIKE A WINNARD: Rumped up, cold, poorly.

MAZED: Angry or all over the place. Confused.

MODGED: Mixed up. A mixed unsightly mess.

NEW VANG*: a novelty of some kind; a new practice or pastime.

NESTLE-BIRD*: the last of a brood whether it be person, pig or bird.

OGGY: Cornish pasty.

ON THE LOP: Never at home, always gadding about.

OPE WAY: Alley way or short cut.

OP*: an ope way, "He've gone up Shilly-alley-op"

PASEL: A group. "here comes a pasel of kids"

PIKE: A pitchfork. A two pronged long handled fork mostly used for handling Hay or Straw.

PUMPSHIP*: to urinate, make water.

PUTHER: See Smeech.

RANDICLE*: a long-winded, complicated story.

REAM*: the top of the milk which has settled (not the cream which is the real scalded or clotted cream) or the surface of the sea, "The pilchards are all up on the ream"

RORA-TORY*: brash coloured, colours not seemly.

SAFE: An outdoor cupboard with perforated zinc walls and door used to keep perishables fresh before fridges became common place.

SCATT: Broken or scattered. Also knock over "scat it flying". Also Gone Scat "gone bankrupt/broke"

SCLOW*: a lovely word to describe a cat scratching your hand or leg as it tries to escape: not just scratching, but digging in the claws.

SCRAGG: To pounce on and overcome an opponent in a friendly way.

SCRAM: To squeeze an item into something which is not really big enough to take it. A lady scrams into a dress which is a size too small.

SEGS: The nails used in hobnail boots.

SHENT or SHANT: A combination of Shall and Not. As in "no I shant be fishing tonight"

SHINK: A combination of "Should" and "Think". As in "I shink that boat is 100 years old"

SIFTER: A small metal shovel used for adding coal to, or removing ash from, an open coal fire.

SKIT: Fizzy drink. A bottle of skit.

SKIFFY: Light rain. Drizzle is skiffy.

SLEEP: Irremovable brown or black marks, usually spots, on clothe which has been stored damp. Clothes go to sleep. Similar to foxing on paper.

SLIPPER: Slippery – Like on eel or an icy road.

SLIPPER: Filthy dirty. Usually clothes or a room. Like the clothes of a tramp that have gone shiny with dirt.

SMEECH: A smoke haze, usually from burnt cooking or the blowback from an open coal fire.

SOUR SABS: The name for Sorrel because of the bitter taste of its leaves.

SOWPIGS: Wood lice.

SPERTICLE*: a naughty, mischievous little boy, a sperticle.

SPLAT: Usually squash or squashed. You can splat a tomato if you stand on it.

SPLIT: A small **s**weet bread bun traditionally used in Cornwall for Jam and Cream not scones.

SQUAL pronounced SQUAAAAL: To cry. "That child is always squaalling."

STAGGED: Same as Lampered. Filthy dirty, covered in mud.

STAGGED OUT: More work than you can cope with.

STARE LIKE A STAT: - look at something you can' t quite understand or can't take your eyes off something.

SSSH: (A sharp intake of breath) :This means Yes. " Is the Earth round?" to which the answer is "SSSH"

STROIL*: couch grass roots, the curse of allotment holders.

TAB: A chunk of grass skimmed off by a BUDIX.

TATIE*: potato.

TEESY: Ill tempered, irritable. Often used to describe fractious children

THAYME: They are. "Thayme forcasting snow tomorrow"

TIG or OFF GROUND TIG: Games of chase and tag played when we were kids. Off the ground you could not be tagged.

TRALLYBASH: Items scattered about randomly, usually junk.

TREADIRON: A bicycle, push bike

UGLY*: foul tempered, angry. "He's in an ugly mood today"

VARMINT: Same as Arab above. Also an ill-tempered woman, and nasty as well.

WRANNY*: a wren

WISH'T: Sickly, Poorly, Unwell, Not very strong. Often used in the phrase "wish't as a winnerd"

WINNERD: a Mistle Thrush.

ZACKLY: affirmative agreement or perfect.

Gorran Haven from an old postcard